Modern Architecture in Japan
Manfredo Tafuri

Edited by Mohsen Mostafavi

7   *Sight Unseen: Manfredo Tafuri and Modern Architecture in Japan*
    Mohsen Mostafavi

19      Introduction

27   I   Relations between European avant-garde art movements and Japanese figurative culture

35   II  Modernization in Japan in the nineteenth and early twentieth centuries
         1. The process of westernization and the first examples of modern architecture in Japan
         2. Practical experience in the 1930s

63   III Postwar architecture
         1. The reconstruction years
         2. Kenzō Tange's early works
         3. Mature rationalism (1953–57)
         4. The first results of the new direction: Tokyo City Hall and the Sogō Department Store
         5. The new school of Japanese architecture
         6. Kenzō Tange
         7. Kunio Maekawa and the MID group
         8. Junzō Sakakura
         9. Current architecture (1957–63)

167  IV  Japanese urban planning
         1. Urban reality and the Tokyo general zoning plan
         2. The Metabolists and the Neo-Mastaba group
         3. Tange's plans for Boston and Tokyo

| | |
|---|---|
| 195 | Conclusion |
| 201 | Selected Bibliography |
| 205 | List of Illustrations |
| | |
| 213 | *Manfredo Tafuri and Architectural Culture in Italy*<br>Marco Biraghi |
| 221 | *Tafuri's Japanese Legacy in Italy—or its Absence*<br>Federico Scaroni |
| 229 | *The Knight's Move*<br>Catherine Ingraham |
| 235 | *Tafuri and Japan: Personal Recollections of Trajectories That Never Crossed*<br>Hajime Yatsuka |
| 243 | *Manfredo Tafuri's Project Japan*<br>Ken Tadashi Oshima |
| 255 | Contributors |

# SIGHT UNSEEN: MANFREDO TAFURI AND MODERN ARCHITECTURE IN JAPAN
## MOHSEN MOSTAFAVI

> Everything we do is but a larva of our intention...
> —Peter Weiss, *Marat/Sade*

Manfredo Tafuri's guide to modern architecture in Japan was published in 1964, when he was twenty-nine years old. He wrote the book during a period of transition, from being a young architect and writer in Rome to becoming a historian of architecture in Venice, where he would eventually assume the chair of architectural history at IUAV, the university's institute for architecture. Tafuri's guidebook—written when he had not yet traveled to Japan—predates the first major articulation of his ideas on architectural history, *Teorie e storia dell'architettura* (Theories and History of Architecture), from 1968. That book introduces topics such as "modern architecture and the eclipse of history" and "architecture as metalanguage." Most famously, it takes aim at "operative criticism," which Tafuri sees as eliminating the necessary divide between the writing of history and the contemporary practice of architecture. He argues that "operative criticism *plans* past history by projecting it towards the future. Its verifiability does not require abstractions of principle, it measures itself each time against the results obtained, while its theoretical horizon is the pragmatist and instrumental tradition."[1]

The same weariness with the instrumental use of history as an aid in design practice is already evident in *Modern Architecture in Japan*. Presumably this was something Tafuri was witnessing first-hand in the work of his contemporaries. In other ways, however, the book is not exactly aligned with his later position—or style. Although a dose of polemics is unavoidable with Tafuri, the book is distinctly less polemical than what was to follow. It is written more in the form of an essay, a continuous text that allows for argument and counterargument. Compared to his later work, the language is also more direct and accessible.

Years after the publication of the guidebook, Tafuri finally went to Japan. The purpose of the trip, during the heyday of postmodernism, was for him to talk about Italian architecture. Still, Tafuri's response to the direct experience of Tokyo and its buildings appears to have been somewhat disinterested; he was not inspired to return to the topic of Japanese architecture. Perhaps the idea and the image of the architecture—sight unseen—appealed to him more than the actual physical artifact. Or perhaps it was more that the style of this small book represented a form of architectural writing that he had turned against. "There is no such thing as criticism; there is only history," he would later say in an interview. "What usually is passed off as criticism, the things you find in architecture magazines, is produced by architects, who frankly are bad historians."[2]

1   From the English edition: Manfredo Tafuri, *Theories and History of Architecture*, trans. Giorgio Verrecchia (New York: Harper & Row, 1980), 141.
2   Interview with Tafuri published in *Design Book Review*, no. 9 (Spring 1986): 8–11.

*Modern Architecture in Japan* is, in fact, as much about criticism as it is about history, and despite its reliance on secondary sources and its occasional inaccuracies, it remains a major contribution to a topic on which there is a lack of significant scholarship, even now. Even at this early stage of his career, Tafuri managed not only to present a clear and coherent formulation of his appreciation of modern Japanese architecture, but also to place it within a broader international context. Equally impressive is his capacity to assemble and configure an incredibly diverse range of references, architects, and buildings, and to discuss the architecture in such detail and with so much conviction. Tafuri does not hold back his opinions or his capacity for description.

Tafuri's book was the first in a series of publications on contemporary architecture under the direction of Leonardo Benevolo. By then in his early forties, Benevolo was already well known for his Storia dell'architettura moderna (History of Modern Architecture, 1960), which went through many reprints and became immensely popular as a textbook, even outside Italy. For his new series, Benevolo commissioned an emerging group of architects, planners, and historians, among them several of Tafuri's friends and collaborators. Spanning from Soviet architecture to Brazilian modernism, from France to the United States, via Germany, Austria, and Great Britain, the series as a whole constitutes a substantial body of knowledge on postwar architecture. Running throughout is a sense of collaboration and debate between a younger generation of writers.

The 1960s was a period of intense debate, even conflict, concerning architecture as a discipline. Tafuri's later critical reflections on the role of history stem in part from his opposition to the teleological approach of Bruno Zevi, professor of architectural history in Venice and one of the most established architectural historians of his day. Zevi's writings, especially his championing of organic architecture, were a point of reference for many contemporary discussions. Tafuri condemned Zevi's "operative criticism," his framing of a direct relationship between history and design, but at the same time acknowledged Zevi's importance for his intellectual development, even referring to him in relation to Japanese architecture. During this period, in addition to Zevi, Tafuri's work engaged with figures such as the art historian Giulio Carlo Argan; Ernesto Rogers, editor of *Casabella-continuità* and partner in the firm BBPR; and the architect and teacher Ludovico Quaroni. Tafuri had been taught by Argan, mentored by Rogers, and was a teaching assistant to Quaroni. His first book, published the same year as *Modern Architecture in Japan*, would be on Quaroni and the development of modern architecture in Italy. Tafuri was both accepting and critical of these influences as he tried to move swiftly from practice to an academic career.

*Modern Architecture in Japan*, then, is not just an analysis of the work of Japanese architects but a critical response to the situation in Italy and beyond. Tafuri argues that the "difficult years" of the modern movement have come to an end, opening the way for new forms of experimentation for building, as well as new directions for thinking about the city. In the context of Japan, he identifies three significant areas of interest. The first involves the relation between what he calls "ideologies and working methods"; the second, the symbolic and communicative role of language; and the third, the relation between architecture and the scale of the emergent city. Even though Tafuri does not include it in this list, he also appreciated the subtle ways in which modern architecture in Japan dealt with the complex issue of tradition, or the connections between the past and the present. The main issue for Tafuri, however, concerns how Japanese architecture responds in specific and productive ways—"with an open mind and considerable energy"—to many of the same questions that confront Italian architecture and the wider international scene. He identifies this reflexive process as the "continual self-criticism and permanent historicization of one's own outlook." According to Tafuri, this is an important and necessary form of action which is not limited to architecture but encompasses the whole of culture.

It is hoped that Modern Architecture in Japan, now translated into English for the first time, will make Tafuri's reflections accessible to a wider audience, including those in Japan. Tafuri begins his presentation of contemporary architecture in Japan with a discussion of the influence of Japanese figurative art on European avant-garde art movements. He could have easily started the book with the following chapter, which describes the process of westernization following the Meiji Restoration in 1868, but by beginning in this way he underscores the reciprocal relationships between Japan and Europe. Tafuri's discussion of the impact of Japanese art is indebted to the writings of Carlo Ragghianti, a prolific Italian art historian whose interest in the concept of "pure visibility" was derived from Benedetto Croce and Konrad Fiedler. This aesthetic theory emphasizes the primary role of sensorial experience—as opposed to verbal language—in shaping our understanding of the world. It argues that to know an image or an object we need to focus on its "pure visibility," which can in turn unlock connections with other senses such as touch or smell.

Tafuri uses Ragghianti's analytical diagram of the portrait James McNeill Whistler painted of his mother (albeit printed the wrong way round in the Italian edition) and the work of Aubrey Beardsley, among others, to make the link between western art and traditional Japanese or "eastern compositions in abstract graphic terms." Another of Tafuri's references on the reciprocities between Japan and Europe involves the connections between Bruno Taut, the German architect who lived in Japan from 1933 to 1936, and Tetsurō Yoshida, the Japanese architect who studied in Germany from 1931 to 1932 and wrote several books on Japanese architecture for a European audience. Tafuri reproduces from Yoshida's *Das Japanische Wohnhaus* (The Japanese House, 1935) a drawing of a series of types of shelving and storage systems. This image of one of the key elements of a Japanese domestic interior recalls Taut's own fascination with variations of color and detail, such as the typological diversity of the doors at his Hufeisensiedlung in Berlin (1925–33).

Having addressed the connections between Japan and the west in the first two chapters, Tafuri then embarks upon the main topic of the book: the history of postwar architecture. The discussion is anchored around the figure of Kenzō Tange and his trajectory, but it also considers the work of two other masters of Japanese modern architecture: Kunio Maekawa and Junzō Sakakura. Tafuri ends the chapter with an analysis of "current architecture" from 1957 up to 1963. While this time frame accommodates the work of the Metabolists, it excludes the architecture of the 1964 Tokyo Olympics (which coincided with the book's publication) and means that Tafuri missed the opportunity to review Tange's masterpiece, the Yoyogi National Gymnasium. The final chapter of *Modern Architecture in Japan* is dedicated to urban planning and seamlessly continues with Metabolism as well as other urban projects from the late 1950s and early 1960s. Tafuri seems less concerned with the nuances of Metabolism as a movement than he is with the proposals of its members. He focuses in particular on Tange's project for Boston Harbor, produced while teaching at MIT, and his well-known Plan for Tokyo.

Manfredo Tafuri's text is explicitly supportive of the innovative achievements of Japanese architecture, seeing in it a coherence—and, most of all, a level of integration of social and architectural intentions—that was unmatched in Europe at the time. Perhaps as a reminder to his European contemporaries, Tafuri ends the book with a double warning, introduced through the words of Giulio Argan. First, he warns against the attempt to revive, unmodified, the constructivist project of rationalism, given that the hopes and ideals that had originally accompanied it had been "mercilessly destroyed by the events of history." Then, perhaps in another reference to his disagreement with Zevi's promotion of organic architecture, he alerts his readers to the pitfalls of pursuing the myth of "spontaneity" —the "revival of an organic unity of being." Instead, Tafuri returns to Argan, who in a manner reminiscent of both Ragghianti and Croce refers to the image as the primary tool of understanding. In these terms, the image is invariably a symbolic "means of reconnecting with an experience of the past that is replete with constructive potential for the future." And it is the articulation of the links to tradition and its projective capacities that Tafuri sees as one of the lasting contributions of modern architecture in Japan.

This volume, in addition to the translation of Tafuri's text, includes a series of contributions by a diverse range of scholars. The aim of these short reflections is to situate Tafuri's writings on Japanese architecture within the broader context of his reception in Italy, the intersections between Italy and Japan, his reception in Japan and then in the US. They also address the complexities of writing about Japan sight unseen, and without the scholarly and historical grounding that Tafuri argued for in his later writings.

However, one thing that Tafuri's guidebook does not lack is the force of his interpretive powers, even in this early stage of his career as a writer and scholar. Since his death, the orthodoxy of Tafuri's position on operative criticism and other topics has increasingly been called into question. The result is the formulation of multiple representations and positions, including the neglect of his work. In that context, the structure of his thinking on Japanese architecture provides valuable insights on the status of criticism in architecture. This period of Tafuri's work also reveals a certain degree of hesitation, even doubt, that adds force to his interest in the conflictual conditions of his métier as a historian. Introducing the second Italian edition of *Theories and History of Architecture,* Tafuri acknowledges the things that remain unsaid and incomplete. For him, the work represents only a first step toward defining what architecture as an institution had meant up to then and suggesting what is yet to come in terms of its relations to modern production processes and capitalist society.

*Theories and History of Architecture* begins with a quote from the play *Marat/Sade* (1964) by the German-Swedish writer Peter Weiss. To the Marquis de Sade's words, "Everything we do is but a larva of our intentions," Jean-Paul Marat replies:

> We must pull ourselves out of the ditch
> by our boot-straps
> turn inside-out
> and see everything with new eyes…

*Modern Architecture in Japan* might also be seen as the outcome of a similar set of contradictory yet evolving thoughts—on the one hand as a "larva" in search of transformation and maturity of ideas, and on the other as a means to see things with new eyes.

# MANFREDO TAFURI

# MODERN ARCHITECTURE IN JAPAN

# INTRODUCTION

For some years now, the idea has been circulating among architectural historians and critics, especially in Italy, that contemporary architecture and urban planning have reached a crucial turning point. And yet until a few years ago you could find the same experts painstakingly exploring the reasons for the crisis in the modern movement, or else defending its enduring validity while remaining resigned to the advent of a long period of more or less abundant and pondered mannerism.

Today, these critical positions appear outdated and unfounded. The modern movement's "difficult years" appear to have concluded with the prospect of still unexplored new horizons, as the most advanced research on construction techniques and, even more significantly, on the new dimension of the city, have gone beyond the "poetics of crisis" to indicate a way forward for new methodologies. At the same time, we need to recognize that we have reached a critical stage, full of potential but also risk, in which thorough, substantial historicization has an indispensable role to play in architectural practice.

The subject of the current volume should therefore be seen against the backdrop of these broader issues. Indeed, the story of Japanese architecture and its most recent developments take on greater significance if considered as part of a general discourse encompassing the whole panorama of international architecture.

One topic requiring special attention is the set of themes that leading Japanese architects seem to have devoted the best part of their energies to over the last decade: the relationship between ideology and working method; language as a means of symbolic communication; and the problem of the "city" as defined in the recent studies of the most radical groups.

From this we see that all the burning issues in the contemporary international discourse have a particularly forceful presence on the Japanese architectural scene. Working with an open mind and considerable energy, Japanese architects seem constantly to come up with concrete solutions to problems that western culture has raised, arguably with greater critical acumen, but has found much more difficult to resolve in practice.

On closer examination, the three broad issues in Japanese architecture summarized above are actually three aspects of a single problem: the problem of language is reducible to the substance of that language, whereas the search for tools and ideologies to address the new scale of urban intervention remains a response to the fundamental question of the meaning of architectural practice in modern society and the role of architecture as a progressive, independent element in the development of culture and civilization.

In ranging from "language" to the "city," the more radical young Japanese architects have adopted an approach to experimentation that is integrated and, to a degree unknown in other non-European and European countries, also homogeneous, both in terms of the type of problems they tackle and the solutions they propose.

Indirectly, then, Japan has made its own contribution to the question of *mannerism*. Here we need to underline the importance of this phenomenon in relation to the type of tradition from which the whole of modern Japanese culture has emerged. But this opens up a new debate that is of great importance, both for its methodological lessons, and for the opportunity it offers to assess the specific contribution of Japanese architecture to the development of the worldwide modern movement. Here again, however, we are faced with two interlocking aspects that are difficult to address in isolation: without doubt, on the international architectural scene—where we have seen on the one hand the vital seeds of new possibilities for action, and on the other considerable involution—the Japanese approach may appear disconcerting, whether on account of its homogeneous character, or its vigorous reaffirmation of civic ideals and social aims at all levels of the project, at a time when international architecture is noted for having "precision of means and confusion of ends."

Following a path that is fraught with obstacles, laborious, and often contradictory, the young Japanese avant-garde has established a historical method as the basis for its experimentation. The continual criticism and ongoing historicization of one's own position is—we repeat—an essential condition not only for architects but for the whole of a culture.

In Japanese architecture in recent years the problem of *tradition* has been posed as a question of historical assessment and critical synthesis. The methodological process, far from taking the memories of a glorious bygone past as "models" to be inserted into a modern repertoire of forms, looks to the illustrious Japanese tradition as a testament, a historical matrix of social structures that modern man must reassess and express in his own well-considered way. Thus, Kenzō Tange and Kunio Maekawa offer the inhabitants of modern Japan living spaces

Fig. 1
Kenzō Tange,
Nichinan
Cultural Center

or "monuments" that are themselves historical judgments: stark, with a violence of expression, but charged too with allusions to the construction methods or exemplars of traditional architecture. Time and again, they refer to the meaning of the relation they establish with history, their distance or proximity to historical processes.

In this approach, architects are undoubtedly helped by the capacity of Japanese society to grasp the nuances inherent in a symbolic discourse around architecture in general and oriental architecture in particular. This is why things that may at first glance seem ingenuous or out of place to us—such as, for example, the structural or wall solutions that echo forms typical of traditional timber architecture, or the configurations that appear to be based on famous historical models—are, in reality, an immediate and direct way of establishing an open and fruitful dialogue with their public, both building users and citizens.

And if in some cases the artifice is too obvious and falls short, the powerful expressiveness and compositional audacity of the best examples constitute a methodological model and point of reference with an international reach. Japanese architecture has, in fact, "accepted the risks of a partial break," as Leonardo Benevolo wrote:

> firmly shifting the emphasis from form to content, and bringing to the fore the concern for social innovation inherent in the modern movement with an enthusiasm that seems to have dulled in the west ... Continuity with tradition was no longer a basic prejudice but a possible point of arrival, insofar as the old values could be retained in the new forms of society.[1]

Precisely because it has inverted the problem of continuity with history in this way, Japanese architecture today offers one

---

[1] Leonardo Benevolo, *Storia dell'architettura moderna* (Laterza: Bari 1960), vol. 2, 1019. English edition, *History of Modern Architecture*, trans. H. J. Landry (Cambridge, MA: MIT Press, 1977), vol. 2, 782.

of the best examples of an authentic, effective solution to the problem of the relation to tradition, an issue that the modern movement has not yet fully resolved.

These are the reasons why international critics are following with growing interest developments in Japanese architecture—an architecture flourishing in a country that endured, in rapid succession, a series of violent civilizational crises that undermined both its traditional and its fast-developing new structures; where there is an ongoing violent struggle between democratic popular movements and the forces of expanding capital; where we see the coexistence, in all its contradictions, of rapid, and consequently hard to control, transformation, and the not inconsiderable burden of anachronistic institutions and customs. In this situation, Japanese culture is making a great effort to offer an independent contribution to civilization, energetically indicating the nature of the specific tasks that require intellectual commitment today.

The modern movement in Europe and the US, worn down by the drama of history, set back several times, is on the way to recovery but finding it extremely difficult to maintain quality while scaling up production to meet the demands of our new, rapidly evolving reality. The "renaissance" of Japanese architecture—as one American critic called it as early as 1959—offers some answers in this regard.[2] But this kind of generic interest, which could be harmful if pursued indiscriminately, needs to be supplemented by a deeper search for content, rooted in the demands raised by the cultural revolutions of our century.

Jean-Paul Sartre recently wrote:

> For the first time, thanks to the struggle for independence and sovereignty being pursued by the underdeveloped nations, history has become truly universal. This is true of

2 Russell Bourne, "Renaissance in Japan," *Architectural Forum*, September 1959: 96–106.
3 Jean-Paul Sartre, "La guerra fredda e l'unità della cultura," *Rinascita*, no. 23 (1962): 26.

the whole range of human activities and it is necessarily also true of culture, which is the expression of them (or rather, is constituted by the same activities insofar as they are signifiers and signified). On the basis of the real unity of history, the contradictory unity of culture will be built.[3]

Forging a contradictory unity, bringing together cultures of different origins and histories, particularly the east and the west, is not just an intellectual or "modish" pursuit but a deep-seated impulse in all areas of European culture (think of Mondrian and Klee, or of Wols and Mathieu), which today must be guided toward an effective, productive synthesis.

# I RELATIONS BETWEEN EUROPEAN AVANT-GARDE ART MOVEMENTS AND JAPANESE FIGURATIVE CULTURE

As is well known, from the mid-nineteenth century on, the pursuit of a synthesis of eastern and western artistic cultures, driven by a variety of visions and conceptions, opened up hitherto unexplored horizons, both figurative and conceptual.

The exchange relations between the two diverse cultures, between east and west, varied according to the specific perspective adopted in the exchanges and the context in which they took place. Altogether, however, they played a not insignificant role in the birth of modern art. Here I will attempt a critical analysis, albeit a very brief one, of the story of those cultural relations as they were forged in nineteenth-century European figurative art.

Examining the reasons for the interdependence of eastern and European art movements in the nineteenth century, Carlo Ragghianti raised the question of how far back those interrelations went:[4]

> Is it true what Pevsner contends,[5] and has often been repeated, that Chinese and Japanese art attracted interest for their synthesis of ornamental and "Impressionistic" features, for their unshaded light, linear and chromatic concision, and decorative stylization of every line and every surface? In short, for values that had already been appreciated in eighteenth-century exoticism and chinoiserie? But, from Baudelaire onward, arabesque and color were effectively the features that made Japanese paintings and engravings desirable items, studied and collected by art critics, connoisseurs, and writers. Oft-cited examples of *japonisme* include the works of Whistler, Degas, Ensor, Van Gogh, Cassatt, Bonnard, Vuillard, Toulouse-Lautrec, Monet, and Toorop. All of these artists were attracted to the features of Japanese graphic art: compositions of oblique or diagonal lines, the truncated "instantaneous" cut of the images (often due, however, to a knowledge of a single print detached from original diptychs and triptychs), the abrupt shifts in scale, the juxtaposition of different planes without a focal perspective, and the use of silhouettes but especially of contours as a form of decorative simplification that also created lively and captivatingly condensed images. Furthermore, from around 1880 on, Felix Régamey and Auguste Lepère specialized in reproducing the techniques and style of Japanese silkscreen printing, while there were also cases of out-and-out imitations, such as Henry Rivière's *The Wave* (1890).

[4] See Carlo L. Ragghianti, *Mondrian e l'arte del XX secolo* (Milan: Edizioni de Comunità, 1962), in particular the chapter "Il contenuto storico della sintesi matura: L'architettura dell'Estremo Oriente."

[5] Nikolaus Pevsner, *Pioneers of the Modern Movement from William Morris to Walter Gropius* (London: Faber & Faber, 1936).

It was not just the taste for line and contour and arabesque, however, that drove the revival of interest in eastern art: western culture, more or less consciously and consequentially, explored the compositional rhythms, the asymmetrical scansions, in Japanese plans and grids, seeking a series of motifs that went beyond straightforward figurative emulation.[6]

Having brought about a revolution in European art, the painters conventionally labelled "Impressionists" (and later the architects of the early modern movement) found confirmation of their ideas and new stimuli in a historically consolidated artistic tradition. For them, it served as both a critical and an operative instrument, able to offer canons and repertoires for elements already present in their own research fields. Beyond this, there were many painters toward the end of the nineteenth century who studied oriental art as a way of recovering the lost ethos of primitive and medieval art, and who pursued medievalism as the expression of a collective popular art.

In different ways, James McNeill Whistler (figs. 2 and 3) and Aubrey Beardsley interpreted traditional eastern compositions in abstract graphic terms. This is also true of the work of British and Dutch illustrators, not least Walter Crane and William Morris (and by extension the Arts and Crafts movement). The enthusiasm for orthogonal grids and multiple divisions is also found in the paintings of Toulouse-Lautrec, Seurat, and Signac, not to mention the revivals at the end of the century by Bonnard and Vuillard, who ostentatiously reproduced the modulations and frames of Kitagawa Utamoro and Japanese textiles.

Moreover, from 1856 Félix Bracquemond's etchings helped to popularize the taste for Japanese prints. Emporia selling Japanese art objects were opened by Madame Desoye in Paris and Murray Marks in London. Initially patronized by intellectuals, they soon fueled a more superficial, commercial fashion for the

[6] The eighteenth- and nineteenth-century trend for exoticism had, however, implicitly opposed the poetics of the "primitive" to "French taste" and rationalism. Thus the impetus to broaden European cultural horizons through contact with Asian civilizations was combined with the desire to rediscover the fountainhead of both the Indo-European languages and the Aryan race.

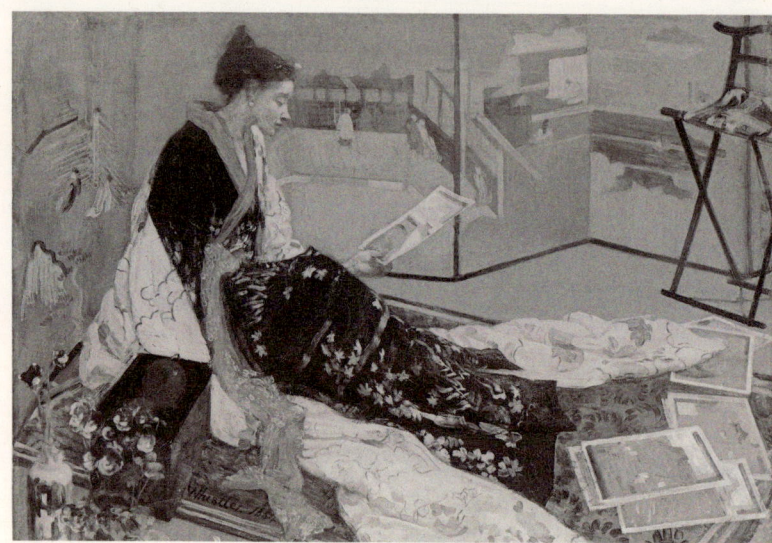

Fig. 2
James McNeill Whistler, *Caprice in Purple and Gold: The Golden Screen*, 1864

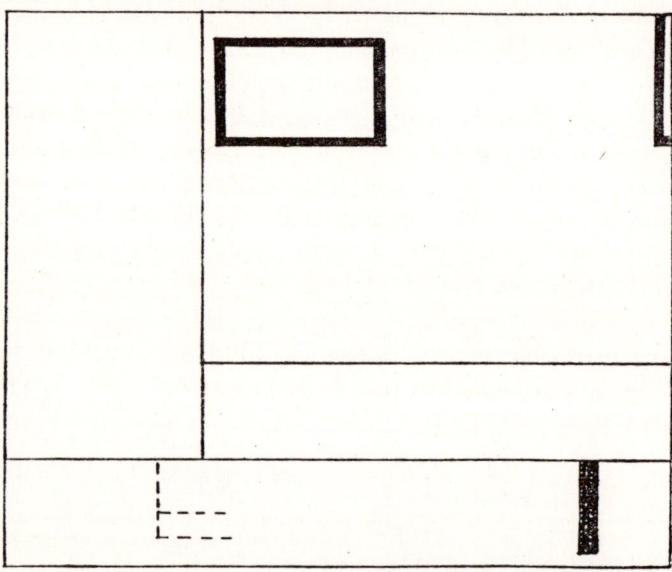

Fig. 3
James McNeill Whistler, *Arrangement in Grey and Black No. 1 (Whistler's Mother)*, scheme

exotic, appealing to the less highbrow demands of the middle class, who approached *japonisme* as one of many such "styles" to be absorbed into their eclectic repertoires. We should distinguish, then, between orientalism as a fashion and the artist's much more profound need to find new viewpoints on figuration (but also, and above all, new moral viewpoints). In this search, the rich, glorious tradition of the far east provided, as we have already noted, concrete logical arguments for historicization.

"If I have to judge what I have seen"—commented Louis Gonse, author of the first complete history of Japanese art, in 1880—"I would have to admit that the cult of Japanese art opened up new horizons for European aesthetics and the further I penetrated the art of Japan, the better I understood some of the great, beautiful works of our own artists."[7]

What happened in painting was soon to be repeated in architecture, again mediated by graphic art and artists like Crane, Morris, and Beardsley as well as Art Nouveau. But rather than reviving or interpreting modulations and grids, the emphasis was now on mining a source of syntactical or linguistic elements. We have only to consider the compositional trend for flat surfaces, whether highlighted, as in the almost linear drawing style of Charles Rennie Mackintosh, or verging on abstraction, as in the work of Otto Wagner (fig. 4) and Josef Hoffmann. Frank Lloyd Wright, as is well known, also explicitly declared his debt to Japanese architecture, seeing in it an adherence to naturalism that reflected some important motifs of his own poetics.[8]

As Decio Gioseffi has suggested, and Ragghianti further elaborated, the experience of Japanese modularity was an important part of Mondrian's thinking: alongside geometric ratios and "dynamic symmetry," the artist also used the method of creating multiple variations on a formal theme through different combinations of constituent elements.[9] Some freer but no less profound relations informed the pedagogy of Johannes Itten at

---

[7] Quoted in Antonio Hernandez, "Die Rolle Ostasiens in der europäischen Kunst," *Werk*, no. 10 (1962): 342.

[8] Frank Lloyd Wright, *An Autobiography* (1932; London: Faber & Faber, 1945), 173.

Fig. 4
Otto Wagner,
Entrance to
Karlsplatz
Metro Station,
Vienna

the Bauhaus, or the painting of Paul Klee and the architecture of Adolf Loos.

In short, the relationship with the legacy of the methodologies of eastern art accompanied the whole development of modern western art. This may have happened with varying degrees of critical awareness, and not always with an adequately framed clarity of purpose, but even the less significant aspects of the phenomenon should not be neglected, since they too are evidence of an enduring latent need imposed by history.

We will now move on to analyze the process just described in reverse: that is, the sweeping westernization of Japanese culture and customs.

9   See Ragghianti, *Mondrian,* and Decio Gioseffi, *La falsa preistoria di Piet Mondrian e le origini del neoplasticismo* (Trieste: Istituto di Storia dell'Arte Antica e Moderna, 1957); see also *Sele Arte*, no. 10 (1957): 10.

# II MODERNIZATION IN JAPAN IN THE NINETEENTH AND EARLY TWENTIETH CENTURIES

1. The process of westernization and the first examples of modern architecture in Japan

While in the west the repertoire of Chinese and Japanese art was being used as a reference point or ideal model for renewal, in Japan, as a consequence of the political revolution enacted by the young Emperor Meiji, western architecture was introduced from 1868 on as a part of a vast project of modernization and westernization pursued by the new government.

We must not underestimate (or for that matter overestimate) this phenomenon of artistic renewal, a consequence of the real political upheaval that accompanied the rise to power of the new emperor after centuries of reactionary and conservative policies under the de-facto rulers, the shoguns and the feudal lords. Much more farsighted than the old military class, the new aristocracy realized that the country would be brutally divided if persisted in its political and socio-economic traditionalism, with unpredictable consequences both at home and with regard to its relations with the western powers.

As Nathaniel Peffer put it:

> There has been something unnatural in Japan's development almost from the start, something that has made the Japanese perhaps a psychologically unhealthy people. The normal advance of any people from the primitive to the civilized is slow, so slow as to be imperceptible at any one time. It is evolution rather than change, and only after the passing of centuries can the difference between one stage and another be detected. It has not been so with the Japanese. They have twice in their history made sudden leaps from one stage to another, leaps spanning centuries: once when they passed in a short period from the near primitive to one of the highest forms then known to man, the Chinese; and again in the nineteenth century, when they passed directly from a medieval, military feudalism to the world of modern science and free inquiry.

Consequently, a Japanese man:

> inhabited simultaneously two worlds, two worlds on wholly different levels and of irreconcilable spirit and content. His reactions were first of one, then of the other. He was torn within, not wholly of one world or the other, unstable in either, unstable in his whole being. This may account for the Japanese inclination to extremes, for the violent fluctuations in thought and action, for the proneness to crazes and fads to which the Japanese people have been so conspicuously addicted in recent years: fads in political ideas or music or architecture.[10]

The Meiji social revolution was undoubtedly typical of propensity toward extreme courses of action. The old order was no longer tenable, having become anachronistic and counterproductive in its concern to maintain a series of privileges. Much better, then, to bring about a complete renewal in all fields: from the constitution, introduced in 1869 along the lines of the French model, to education, social relations (the Samurai class vanished forever in 1877), and customs. Inevitably, the Meiji restoration was burdened by ambiguity and amateurism. Under the banner of nationalism, the new regime pursued a radical, innovative goal: feudal privileges were abolished, fiefdoms were suppressed and replaced with prefectures (of which the hereditary landowners (*daimyo*) were now appointed governors); freedom of worship and a weekly day of rest were introduced in tandem. Against the rise of a new class of technicians and an enlightened managerial elite, a rigid dirigisme prevailed in the circle of advisors around the emperor. The industrialization of the country, boosted by state subsidies for the major entrepreneurial families, led to a rise in living standards but it also established a capitalist oligarchy in place of the aristocracy of the Imperial Council. When Japan came to draft a new constitution in 1889, it was not by chance that, after carefully examining the systems in several western countries, Prince Ito opted for the most rigid and militarized order: that of Kaiser Wilhelm's Germany. Thus, as the country was strengthened internally, and industrial production began to reach fairly high levels, the old structures that had stood in the way of a policy of expansionism were eliminated. Japan went to war with China from 1894–95 in pursuit of territorial aims and international prestige. By 1932 this drive had degenerated into fanaticism and led to the catastrophe of World War II.

In assessing the renewal of Japan in the 1870s, we need to remember the obverse of this continuous process—the survival

10   Nathaniel Peffer, *The Far East: A Modern History* (Ann Arbor: University of Michigan Press, 1958), 31–32. Peffer's remarks should be borne in mind when considering recent Japanese utopian urbanism, see chapter IV.

of some elements of the old political and social order. The new ruling class's great haste aggravated the amateurism already lamented above, initially giving rise to some naive imitation. To give a marginal but telling example, this could be seen in the change to western-style clothing by the emperor, who even used the same make-up as Napoleon III.

This kind of example was not without consequences in a country in which symbols had a power unknown in the west. Imitation, in fact, became the main objective not only of the new elite, but of the population as a whole. With astonishing energy, fueled by a continuous exchange of teachers and students, the Japanese turned to various European nations, absorbing the models for the particular field of technology or culture in which they excelled: the navy in the case of Britain, law in France, medicine and military art in Germany. As part of this cultural renewal, the Meiji government also sought to reform architecture and construction techniques. After the creation of a building division within the Ministry of Engineering in 1870, architects from various countries were invited to Japan to design new public buildings that could serve as models for local architects on account of their prominent representative character. Among the architects who settled in Japan were the American Richard P. Bridgens, the Englishman Josiah Conder, the Frenchman Charles de Boinville, the Italian Giovanni Vincenzo Cappelletti, and the German Hermann Ende.

The buildings that the European architects designed were highly emblematic. Without exception, they not only adopted the principles of western eclecticism but went to great lengths to apply different styles to emphasize the building's specific representative function. Cappelletti, for example, adopted a medievalesque eclecticism for the Tokyo Museum of History (1881) and a Renaissance style with some Northern European influences for the Imperial General Headquarters the same year (fig. 5). Conder, on the other hand, was considered to be the most interesting architect of the Meiji period, partly because he attempted to adapt the western repertoire to Japanese

Fig. 5
G. V. Cappelletti,
Imperial General
Headquarters,
Tokyo

conditions by introducing far and middle eastern influences in buildings such as the Rokumeikan (1883), a reception center for foreigners, and the Russian Orthodox Church (1891), both in Tokyo.[11]

Japanese architects and the general public thus came into contact with a wide range of western styles and some buildings that were revolutionary in terms of taste. In fact, previously in Japanese there had been no term for, or even concept of, architecture. There were two kinds of designs: *zōka* (building) for residential constructions and *fushin* (a term derived from donations given for the construction of temples). In the latter case the style was dictated by the religious function of the building, regulated by rituals and a rigorous adherence to precedents (figs. 6–8). The western examples imported by European architects met with great interest—so much so that architects and students flocked to the relevant sites to study the design and building methods, which certainly could not be classified according to

11 Few of these buildings have survived. For the architecture of the Meiji period, see K. Abe, "Meiji Architecture," in *Japanese Arts and Crafts in the Meiji Era*, ed. Naoteru Ueno and Richard Lane (Tokyo: Pan-Pacific Press, 1958). See also Eizo Inagaki, "Revolt and Conformity in Architecture," *This is Japan* (the article also appeared in Italian with numerous illustrations in *Casabella continuità*, no. 273 (1963), including the buildings cited here). The Irish civil engineer Thomas James Waters designed some of the first western-style buildings in Japan, among them the Imperial Japanese Mint in Osaka (1871) and, much more importantly, the Ginza district in Tokyo (begun in 1872), clearly modeled on John Nash's Regent Street.

MODERNIZATION IN JAPAN

Fig. 6
Imperial Palace, Tokyo, grand audience gallery

Fig. 7
*Karesansui* garden in Ryōan-ji Temple, Kyoto

Fig. 8
Main hall of the Grand Shrine of Ise

the two traditional categories. Much more than the figurative aspects, the Japanese were interested in the western technologies, which they were keen to absorb as quickly as possible.

This explains the remarkable influence of eclecticism and of European methods of design. The new Imperial College of Engineering, under British direction, offered a practical architecture course from its founding in 1873. Before long, a new cohort of trained Japanese technicians began to replace foreign architects in public building projects.

In the meantime, toward the end of the Meiji period, Japan was undergoing a wholesale industrial revolution driven by the heady rise of capitalism, and bolstered in part by two wars: the Sino-Japanese War of 1894–95 and the Russo-Japanese War of 1904–05. The rise of capitalism and the consolidation of the bourgeoisie, who by then had supplanted the traditional aristocracy in the Imperial Council, gave Japanese architects ample opportunities to apply the assiduously acquired new technologies. In 1895, the construction of a department store saw the first Japanese experiment in the field of steel structures, while the first reinforced concrete structure was built for a Tokyo insurance company in 1912.

These early buildings promised to mark the end of the narrow emphasis on the techniques that had initially dominated Japanese architectural culture. Great efforts were made to popularize the neologism *kenchiku*, coined to correspond to our term "architecture." Nonetheless, they failed to achieve the desired results: *kenchiku* increasingly came to stand for the whole set of construction techniques rather than for the aesthetic value of buildings.[12]

As Leonardo Benevolo comments:

> This shows that the Japanese concept differs from the western one not so much in extent as in the mental framework. Europeans, following the Renaissance concept, had in mind an abstract and general value, concerned with a single aspect of building activity, whereas the Japanese—like the men of the Middle Ages—had in mind a concrete and particular activity, whose various aspects were perceived as a single unified whole.[13]

But at this point a further influx of western influences disrupted not only the technological and functional aspects of this tradition but also the very means of evaluating it. A group of Japanese

---

[12] The word "architecture" was first translated as *zōka* (meaning "house creation") during the early phase of the country's process of westernization. In 1897, Chuta Ito (who is considered the father of modern architecture in Japan) adopted a new term, *kenchiku*, which became the official translation of "architecture." Similar to the word architecture, *kenchiku* can also sometimes mean building or construction [editor's note].

[13] Benevolo, *History of Modern Architecture*, vol. 2, 774. Artists in the earliest days of modernism might have intuitively grasped this unitary aspect without exploring it in theoretical terms.

scholars at the Imperial University undertook a critical revision of the history of Japanese architecture according to European methods, which focused more on the aesthetic qualities of buildings. For this purpose, K. Kigo set up a course on the history of Japanese architecture in 1887 (the first of its kind in the country). Later, C. Itō and T. Sekino would co-found the Institute of Architectural History, which aimed to make a comparative study of the characteristics of both eastern and western architecture.

In essence, the introduction of new building techniques stimulated an interest in the contents of those techniques. After the initial phase of uncritical acceptance, the Japanese began to understand that the revolution in methods of construction needed to be accompanied by an enquiry into the implications of that renewal. It required them to examine their own past to understand the rupture that the new, widely accepted style represented.

The new emphasis on critical studies did not go hand in hand with a change in working methods. If we look at the works of Japanese artists and architects from 1887 to 1920, we find they are merely making use of the eclectic repertoire introduced by western architects without attempting to reinterpret it in their own original way. Kingo Tatsuno's Bank of Japan and Institute of Technology, Yorichika Tsumaki's Tokyo Chamber of Commerce, and Yuzuru Watanabe's Imperial Hotel are among the most impressive works of that period. Ultimately, however, they only really highlight their architects' exceptional talent for imitation.

Small wonder, then, that Japan failed to take heed of the new developments in architecture around the turn of the century in Europe. Too busy making up ground and introspectively exploring their own world, the Japanese did not grasp the scope —and, even more, the particular significance—of modernism. Scant attention was paid to the various movements arising from the revolutions in modern art. A significant example is the almost complete absence of Art Nouveau or Werkbund influences. The modern movement itself was only introduced into Japan toward the end of Taishō period (1912–26).

And yet, the problem of the language of architecture continued to be debated. In a conference at the Japanese Institute of Architecture in 1910, the question of style was on the agenda. Although the topic was presented in a very narrow way, the discussion took an emblematic turn and the issues were extended to the whole life of society. Even in Japan, then, the time was ripe for a new vision of the profession—of the relations between art and ideology and the scope of the architectural intervention.

The most interesting outcome of the 1910 conference, however, was the unanimous stand taken against the passive reproduction of western styles. Though propelled by naive functionalist ideals, the drive for a modern Japanese architecture was beginning to take shape. At this stage, it was limited to a call to graft traditional eastern elements onto imported buildings and technologies, but by the 1930s, under the yoke of the totalitarian regime, the pursuit of aesthetic independence would degenerate into a deplorable nationalism. In 1910 that nationalism not only reflected a considerable inferiority complex; it also revealed an awareness that the traditional style of architecture—like other longstanding forms of tradition—was definitively outmoded, admissible only in an eclectic repertoire.

In the end, writers were quicker than architects to grasp the new dimension introduced by the experiments of the European avant-gardes. Rationalism, first invoked by S. Okada and R. Sano, was taken up by S. Yoshino and a group of intellectuals who promoted it as a new way of living in modern dwellings. This gave rise to the fashion of the *bunka jutaku* (new-style house) which, as Alfred Drexler points out, had positive aspects but usually involved a good dose of cultural snobbery as well.

In parallel, inspired by the development of democratic ideals after World War I and the projects of the international modern movement, a group of young architects led by Kikuji Ishimoto, Sutemi Horiguchi, Mayumi Takizawa, and Mamoru Yamada formed Japan's first avant-garde movement under the name of *Bunri Ha Kenchiku Kai* (Association of Secessionist Architects).

Fig. 9
Frank Lloyd Wright, Imperial Hotel, Tokyo

This was also the period when construction began on Frank Lloyd Wright's Imperial Hotel in Tokyo (1918)—the first work by a master of modern western architecture in Japan. Japanese architects, however, saw the building more as a stimulus for research than a methodological model. Wright himself had borrowed elements from the syntax and construction methods of the eastern tradition, only he used them as symbols, ideograms inserted into a very personal context. For anyone unacquainted with the cultural developments informing Wright's romanticism, their expressionism must have been almost incomprehensible (fig. 9).

Unsurprisingly, the American architect's encounter with Japanese art turned out to be more fruitful for his architecture than for Japan. Wright readily adopted ideas and stimuli from the oriental tradition, finding in them the organic qualities and the relationship with nature that he sought. What he appreciated in Japanese art was "the elimination of the insignificant, a process of simplification," a process he had already embarked on in his own work. He ignored the fact that western and eastern art cannot be measured by the same yardstick (while the term "simplification" can obviously be applied to western art, it has no meaning in relation to eastern art, which for centuries developed in a completely different way).

In his autobiography of 1932, Wright wrote: "Japanese art and architecture really did have organic character. Their art was nearer to the earth and a more indigenous product of native conditions of life and work, therefore more nearly 'modern' than any European civilization alive or dead."[14] Once again a western artist had discovered the value of a tradition that was now mute for the Japanese, who continued to move closer to the language of rationalism.

"In the west"—commented Japanese critic Shinji Koike—"the international expositions were the milestones marking the progress of modern architecture, while in Japan natural calamities provided the opportunity for architectural innovation. The first such calamity was the great Kantō earthquake in September 1923; the second, the large-scale destruction due to World War II."[15] The 1923 earthquake, which almost completely razed Tokyo, enforced a program of reconstruction and, with it, a reassessment of how to build in relation to the country's natural topography and socio-economic conditions. The proponents of the modern movement responded by forming new associations, *Kenchiku Kai* and *Shinkō Kenchikukai Remnei* (Association of Young Architects), and publishing books on architecture and specialist journals. Prof. K. Imai of the University of Waseda was likewise an active propagandist. On a long study trip to Europe he came into contact with Le Corbusier, Gropius, Taut, and Mies and relayed their interests and aims back to Japan.[16]

---

14  Wright, *An Autobiography*, 173. Wright's work did, however, have some direct influence: Arata Endo, for example, who worked as an assistant on the Imperial Hotel, later designed some buildings in which the language is close to that of Wright (see the Jiyu Gakuen School, Tokyo, and the Kōshien Hotel, Osaka).
15  Shinji Koike, *Contemporary Architecture of Japan* (Tokyo, 1953), 16.

The interests of the modern movement were also promoted by the work of two European architects of considerable standing. The Czech-born American Antonin Raymond was the first to settle in Japan in 1920, and he played a prominent role in the field of practice, becoming a reference point for the younger generations who had the opportunity to gain concrete and direct experience in his studio.

In a conversation with Kenzō Tange, Raymond said:

> Imagine my surprise on arriving in Japan to find here expressed in Japanese farms and Shinto shrines like Ise all the features which we so ardently desired to re-create in the new architecture. A Japanese farm at the time of my arrival in Japan forty years ago was a marvel of integration, complete, and perhaps not to be found anywhere else in the world. It grew out of the ground like a mushroom or a tree, natural and true, it developed from the inside function absolutely honestly; all structural members were expressed positively on the outside, the structure itself was the finish and the only ornament, all materials were natural, selected and worked by true artist artisans; everything in it and around it was simple, direct, functional, economical. The people, their dress, their utensils, their pottery, paintings, gardens, all expressed the marvellous unity of purpose clearly developed through the ages by a natural process like anything else in nature. ... It contained absolute principles, which always were and always will be the same, immutable, unchangeable, and which must guide us in trying to attain true beauty in architectural design.[17]

---

16    In the meantime, painting and sculpture underwent a similar process of modernization and westernization. In 1910, the Shirakaba group of writers and artists introduced to Japan the work of Cézanne, van Gogh, Rodin, Bourdelle, and the Post-Impressionists in general. Later the avant-garde group called Nikakai rebelled against the dominant academicism, while by 1920, Cubism, Futurism, and Expressionism were already part of Japanese figurative culture. Lastly, in 1937, Saburō Hasegawa and his group campaigned intensely to spread abstract art.

In this way, Raymond renewed a typically European interest in classical Japanese architecture, which he saw as a significant precursor of the modern movement. The whole of his work was focused on highlighting this cultural affinity.[18]

Bruno Taut, one of the pioneers of the European modern movement, also lived in Japan from 1933 to 1936 and studied Japanese building traditions in relation to the needs and demands of modern life. Taut was the first to realize that the European interest in the Japanese tradition would be fruitless if it limited itself to formal appearances, especially if, in determining which elements could usefully create continuity with the legacy of the past, it made no precise critical distinction between elements which were based on formal allusions as opposed to methodological assumptions (this was a timely warning, particularly for Japanese culture). "Naturally I do not want to contest that locally conditioned peculiarities have a great influence on architecture," Taut wrote in 1935:

> But these are things that can never be understood by a non-Japanese, and therefore remain sterile for the innovation of architecture now being pursued all over the world. I believe, however, that they are also sterile for the further development of Japanese architecture itself.[19]

17   Quoted in James M. Richards, "Japan 1962," *Architectural Review*, no. 787 (1962): 218. The article was republished in Richards' *An Architectural Journey in Japan* (London: Architectural Press, 1963). Raymond's aesthetic evaluations may be seen as an attempt to endow the cult of European modernism with a universal, historicized element of taste.

18   Antonin Raymond was born in 1890 and educated at the University of Prague. In 1910 he moved to the United States, where he worked in Cass Gilbert's practice. After an interlude as a painter in Italy, he spent a year in Taliesin, having been invited there by Frank Lloyd Wright. Raymond returned to Japan after World War I to work on the Imperial Hotel in Tokyo, overseeing the construction together with Wright. He then stayed on in Tokyo and opened his own practice. The house he designed for himself in 1923 was the first building in Japan with an exposed concrete structure. His later works, especially the Chapel for the Tokyo Christian Women's College (1934), were clearly influenced by French architect Auguste Perret. (His assistant, the young Czech Bedrich Feurstein, had been one of Perret's best students.) Raymond returned to the US in 1937, due to the political turmoil in Japan, but would reopen his practice in Tokyo in 1947.

19   Bruno Taut, *Fundamentals of Japanese Architecture* (Tokyo: Kokusai Bunka Shinkokai, 1936), 10. Quoted in Benevolo, *History of Modern Architecture*, vol. 2, 775.

What Taut grasped was the symbolic value of Japanese visual culture. This value corresponds, moreover, to a shared sense of the symbolic characterizing precise moments in Japanese life. The rooms for the tea ceremony (fig. 10) are a good example of this:

> Their beauty—often great—is beyond question, and yet in spite of all its fineness, it is in itself sterile for modern Japan. This is not architecture, but improvised lyricism, so to speak. But lyricism, as in poetry, does not readily convey itself in wood, bamboo, shoji, mats, stucco, and so forth. The old masters of the tea ceremony stressed the unique subjectivity of the pure beauty of this atmosphere. They declared that it would be lost by repetition and they would certainly pronounce all the elements of the tea-house to be 'cheap' ... What was meant to be a unique expression of spiritual personality of a restful character turned into petrified rules and dry academicism—not only in the architectural details but in the tea ceremony itself."[20]

Leaving aside the debatable distinction between architecture and lyrical improvisation (one that is perfectly understandable, however, in the context of 1930s culture), Taut encapsulates the deep contradiction between the demands imposed by new production methods, new techniques, new social relations, and new customs, and a way of life and of building that strives above all to achieve an *unicum* where each repetition is conditioned by a shared world of symbols and by its own refined individualization.

An increasingly urgent, profound change was thus inevitable: the diehard conservatism of the past centuries had opened a yawning gap between the progress of western nations and enduring Japanese feudalism. Once the need to catch up with western culture had been acknowledged, there was no way of

---

20  Taut, *Fundamentals of Japanese Architecture,* 11. Quoted in Benevolo, *History of Modern Architecture*, vol. 2, 775.

Fig. 10
Main hall of
Jo-an Teahouse,
Inuyama

avoiding the break with the past, or at least its more obviously anachronistic aspects.

Within this pursuit of total modernization, historical continuity could only be assured methodologically, by constantly subjecting the new demands in a culture to objective criticism. The importance of Taut's work in the Japanese world therefore lies in his critical contribution. He offered a new scale of values for historical interpretation that differed from the studies by Kigo or Sekino, and even the contributions of other Europeans. For Taut, it was not about the dependence of oriental art on western artistic methods, or about Japanese tradition anticipating European avant-garde figurative theories and methods. Rather, Taut assessed the architecture of Japan in terms of its independent values and explored the possibility of its continuity in the midst of profound social change.

The debate thus began to take on a new shape: the younger generations responded to the critical contributions, and the cultural movements multiplied. The Japanese Association for Industrial Design (Nihon Kōsaku Bunka Renmei), whose members included H. Kishida, S. Horiguchi, K. Ichiwa, K. Maekawa,

Y. Taniguchi, and S. Koike, set out to coordinate the development of modernism in Japan by linking the figurative arts to industrial production. Their journal, *Gendai Kenchiku*, played an important role in disseminating these goals.

By around 1920, Japanese architecture was characterized by a notable American influence, one of the consequences of the political sway of the United States over Japan at that time. The Industrial Bank of Japan by Setsu Watanabe and Gen'itsu Yamazaki (1923) reproduced the classic model of the contemporary American office block. A similar phenomenon can be seen in the Mitsubishi Bank, designed by Shotaro Sakurai and Akira Fujimura, and the Marunouchi Building, designed locally, but constructed by American contractors who used industrialized building systems for the first time in Japan. Not surprisingly, Marunouchi served as a model for many Japanese companies (the two major construction companies, Shimizu and Obayashi, sent observers to the construction site, and Shimizu bought all the equipment used by the American firm).

This phase of indiscriminate adoption of new techniques was evidently a rite of passage that Japanese architecture had to go through, but it would soon give way to a more mature approach to acquisition.

## 2. Practical experience in the 1930s

From 1932 to 1937, young Japanese architects addressed the problem of a new language with incredible energy, producing some remarkable early works. Among them, Sakakura's Pavilion at the 1937 Paris Exposition attracted great international interest, even being rated by Alfred Roth as one of the most significant buildings of the decade.[21]

The works of Horiguchi, Yamaguchi, Togo Murano, and K. Ishimoto achieved, or at least successfully addressed, the long-sought aim of an authentic cultural integration with European movements, although, as Drexler pointed out, conservative tendencies also continued to grow, albeit quietly in the background.[22] These tendencies would experience a triumphant resurgence in 1937, when the authoritarian regime stifled new developments.

But it is precisely the attitude of the nationalistic dictatorship toward the Japanese modern movement that enables us to gauge its validity, given that in all eras the supreme arbiters of the ideological power of art have been the reactionary ruling classes.

The cultural debate prompted by the younger generations was of an uneven standard and often undermined by ambiguity. Alongside Horiguchi, who was undoubtedly the most accomplished architect of that period, there were many others who engaged in eclecticism or passive, indiscriminate imitation. The more fervent advocates of the modern movement, on the other hand, seemed preoccupied with illustrating and experimenting with various international trends.

In this context one of Horiguchi's earliest buildings, the Ōshima Meteorological Station (1928; fig. 11), reveals his deep

---

21   See Alfred Roth, *La nouvelle architecture: Présentée en 20 exemples/Die neue Architektur/The New Architecture* (Zurich: Girsberger, 1940).

22   Drexler cites as a telling example the Honganji Temple in Tokyo (1934): the meaningless eclecticism combines a traditional-style interior with a hotchpotch exterior of Italian Renaissance style, a giant order of columns borrowed from the Indian tradition, and windows echoing the modes of German mannerism. See Arthur Drexler, *The Architecture of Japan* (New York: Museum of Modern Art, 1955), 247.

Fig. 11
Sutemi
Horiguchi,
Ōshima
Meteorological
Station

engagement with the international debate; the form of the complex is limpid, essential, with the link between the high tower and the low blocks recalling a typical Dudokian modulation. This was no random reference, given that Horiguchi, after co-founding the *Bunri Ha Kenchiku Kai,* had traveled around Europe for two years and met many leading architects, including the circles around *De Stijl* and *Wendigen*. On his return from Europe he would publish a book on modern Dutch architecture.

The Dutch influence continued in Horiguchi's Kikkawa House (1930), where the plan, vaguely similar to the complex organizations of traditional dwellings, is extruded into an interesting, if somewhat unwieldy, play of volumes that re-elaborates the language of the International Style in an original way.

Horiguchi would only free himself from this unwieldiness eight years later, with his project for the Wakasa House (1939), one of the most significant examples of prewar Japanese architecture (fig. 12). The Wakasa House restates, in an extremely rigorous way, all the principles of functionalism: *plan libre*, stereometric envelope, and asymmetric disposition of the facades. As a whole, however, it clearly displays a finesse at the expressive level—a softness and even a certain laxness in its use of the vocabulary of rationalism. In Horiguchi, Taut's call for a selective, methodological return to Japanese tradition found a natural, valid interpreter.

A similar formal and aesthetic approach can be seen in the buildings of Yamaguchi, in particular the Tokyo Dental School (1934), or in Mamoru Yamada's Teishin Hospital (1937), one of the finest examples of Japanese architecture from the 1930s in terms of balance and careful, functional design (fig. 13).

Alongside this fairly uniform group of buildings, a number of works by Kikuji Ishimoto and the Sōusha group graft elements of traditional figuration onto a constructionist language rich in neoplastic allusions. Although they sometimes produce interesting motifs, these attempts at synthesis appear either ingenuous or overly crude. Buildings such as Ishimoto's Shirokia Department Store in Tokyo (fig. 14) or the

Fig. 12 Sutemi Horiguchi, Wakasa House, Tokyo

Fig. 13 Mamoru Yamada, Teishin Hospital, Tokyo

Fig. 14
Kikuji Ishimoto,
Shirokia
Department
Store, Tokyo

Fig. 15
Sōusha,
competition
entry for the
Ukrainian
State Theater,
Kharkiv

MANFREDO TAFURI

Sōusha competition project for the new Ukrainian State Theater in Kharkiv (1931) do, however, achieve their own distinctive, somewhat overelaborate expressiveness (fig. 15).

During the great drive to improve working practices in the 1930s, Tetsurō Yoshida was one of the most important contemporary critics, representing what could be seen as the "moderate" current within the Japanese modern movement. While studying in Europe in 1931–32, Yoshida had met Hugo Häring and Ludwig Hilberseimer, who encouraged him to make the history of Japanese architecture better known in the west.

In response to the German architects' request, Yoshida wrote a seminal book on the "Japanese House" that was published by Wasmuth in 1935.[23] In Europe and America, the knowledge it imparted of the Japanese tradition of housing served to confirm the modern movement's aspirations toward simplicity and the use of standard elements (part of western culture thus continued the "alienating" appropriation of complex motifs from Japanese art (fig. 16)). Meanwhile, in Japan, Yoshida's historical survey assumed a different value: concurrent with Taut, this Japanese scholar studied the history of Japanese architecture to grasp the salient, enduring features of a tradition that had been exhausted as a formal repertoire or ritual series of models, but still had the potential to be reinterpreted in its historically realized, demythified, concrete forms.

Yoshida's early works, from Kyōdō Post Office (1922) and Telegraph Office (1926), through Beppu City Hall (1928), to Tokyo Central Post Office (1931) and Osaka Post Office (1939; fig. 17) seem—nevertheless—to aim for a rationalistic monumentality, with echoes of classicism in the display of the structural grid (something redeemed at Osaka by a vigorous approach to the body of the building which anticipates, even in its schematism, a kind of stripped-down brutalism). Yoshida's

---

23   Tetsurō Yoshida, *Das Japanisches Wohnhaus* (Berlin: Wasmuth, 1935). Although not particularly important for the purposes of this volume, the archaic monumentalism of Yoshida's architecture inevitably also reveals a flaw in his approach to historical interpretation.

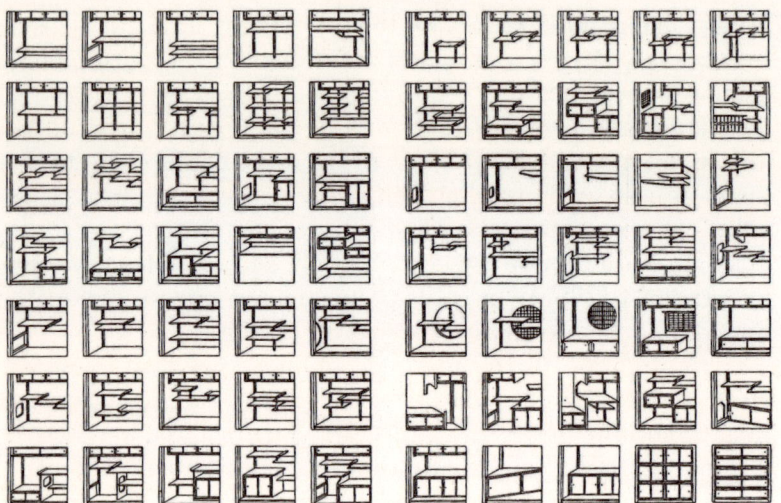

Fig. 16
Tetsurō Yoshida, seventy variations in the composition of *tana* and *tokowaki* shelving

Fig. 17
Tetsurō Yoshida, Osaka Post Office

Fig. 18
Togō Murano,
Sogō Department Store,
Osaka

main contribution to Japanese architectural culture, however, lies in his historical methodology, the importance of which overshadows any practical inconsistencies in his built works.

Undoubtedly the most interesting and complex work by a Japanese architect in the prewar period is the Sogō Department Store in Osaka (1935) by Togō Murano (fig. 18). Murano, who worked for Setu Watanabe up to 1929, was one of the most original exponents of Japanese modern architecture, and the Sogō Department Store is the first expression of his personal style as well as arguably being his masterpiece. Murano makes the department store symbolic of the *concentration* of modern society. But what it represents is not so much an image of capitalist distribution as a community organism in which *exchange* takes place not at a purely commercial level but at a social level as well. In this way Murano's department store becomes a fulcrum of the city, alternating retail spaces with spaces for the community and social institutions. The formulation of the building achieves a jump in scale, with the large department store, the hub of modern urban organization, being linked to the city as a whole and even to the wider region. This defines a new dimension for the city, both formally and functionally, as the primary node of concentration of the population.

There is a strong emphasis on the interior space, the true protagonist of Murano's functional concept, while the external volume, identified as one of the main components in the city structure, acquires its own powerful aesthetic characterization. The unitary nature of the surfaces of the Sogō Department Store—obtained through their dramatic segmentation into a dense series of vertical grooves that generate a continuous play of shadow and light over the whole mass of the building—enters into a dynamic relationship with the urban space and is directly related to it. The breaks created by Y. Fujikawa's sculptures in the vertical block and a low corner block further accentuate the compactness of the building, endowing it with a forceful expressiveness that is exceptional not only in Japanese architecture of the 1930s but in the International Style as a whole.

In Murano's last works we see a further development and strengthening of the innovative ideas expressed in the Sogō Department Store which makes it clear that the Osaka building was not a one-off masterpiece but a key milestone in Japanese architectural history.

In the meantime, two architects from the younger generation, Kunio Maekawa and Junzō Sakakura, had gained extensive first-hand knowledge of Le Corbusier's working methods as apprentices in his Paris atelier: Maekawa in 1928–30 and Sakakura in 1931–36. The direct influence of Le Corbusier's methods would prove crucial for these two designers, as we will see in more detail below. After returning to Japan and completing his training in Raymond's studio, Maekawa opened his own practice in 1925 and tenaciously fought against the first signs of a conservative backlash. In these years he realized a series of important works, including the Hinomoto Civic Center (1936), Showa Metalworking Plant (1937), and Dalian Town Hall (1938)—buildings that already contain the seeds of subsequent developments in his architecture.

Fig. 19
Junzō Sakakura,
Japan Pavilion,
1937 Paris
Exposition

While Maekawa's works remained closely tied to the national debate, Sakakura immediately won international acclaim for his first built project, the Japanese Pavilion at the 1937 Paris Exposition, which was designed during his stay in the city (fig. 19). Sakakura's pavilion was seen as heralding a renewal of Japanese architecture. Though it was not, in fact, the most significant sign of this renewal, its various ingredients—its rationalist organization, its refined treatment of surfaces, and its siting, on a woody hillock accessed by elegantly designed ramps and paths—constituted a very accomplished synthesis of traditionally opposed cultures—or, rather, corresponded to western ideas about the qualities required for such a synthesis.

In any case, the success of Sakakura's pavilion marked the official entry of Japanese architectural culture into the international discourse.

# III POSTWAR ARCHITECTURE

1. The reconstruction years

In the years after the Anti-Comintern Pact with Germany (1936) and the Second Sino-Japanese War (1937), the internal contradictions of Japanese society enabled the rise of an extremely conservative, ultra-nationalistic dictatorship. The whole of Japanese culture came under the direct control of the authorities, and Japanese architecture was subsumed into the Internazionale dei pompieri (Pompiers' International), to use Giuseppe Pagano's phrase.[24] Although the reference to *art pompier* may seem a little out of place, it does capture the chauvinistic return to moribund, bombastic forms.

The Japanese modern movement would only be revived after World War II. In the immediate postwar period, its efforts were focused on the recovery of a population who were still stunned by the catastrophes of Hiroshima and Nagasaki—a suffering population who began the process of reconstruction in a state of unconsciousness, and who only slowly gained a dramatic self-awareness and injection of inspiration.

The initial reconstruction work began under the aegis of the occupying US military forces, which set up a temporary house-building program to replace housing stock destroyed during the war. General MacArthur appointed an American financial expert, Joseph Dodge, to draw up a plan to rebalance the national budget, which the Japanese government immediately signed up to. However, the plan triggered a period of deflation and led to the introduction of strict curbs on spending, drastically limiting construction projects until around 1950.

The economic recovery in 1950 likewise owed more to external factors than internal developments. The Korean War and the political alliance with the United States had the effect of re-energizing all of Japan's industrial infrastructure, bringing fresh aid and subsidies. On the condition of that political alliance, the country regained its sovereignty, and the trade surplus peaked at around three hundred million dollars in the years from 1951 to 1953. Bolstered both economically and psychologically, the Japanese began to regain confidence in their own capacities and rebuild their national pride. The leading role in this recovery was played by the fully re-established stock market. The economy, however, was still run by the same capitalist class—the great industrial entrepreneurs (*zaibatsu*)—who had previously been so closely tied to the military and the dictatorship. Indeed, after the war, the politically powerful industrialists had gone on trial together with the generals. But once again, political expediency led to a change in US policy toward Japan: to

24  Giuseppe Pagano, "Internazionale dei pompieri," *Costruzioni Casabella*, no. 147 (March 1940) [translator's note].

ward off the dangers of a popular democratic revolution, capitalist industrial development was now promoted by every means.[25]

Japan thus entered a new phase characterized by a western influence that was much less controlled or controllable than it had been in the previous century. In this period of new-found well-being and economic growth, the country looked to western nations that had already reached a high level of capitalist development. But as in any country starting out from a state of underdevelopment, there were signs of the internal imbalances, economic and cultural, that typically occur when reconstruction is not governed by overall democratic planning. This can be seen in the work of intellectuals who described, in increasingly dramatic and exasperated terms, a situation of crisis, notwithstanding the economic boom. In literature, Ryūnosuke Akutagawa, Osamu Dazai, Shintaro Ishihara, and the Shin-gesaku group helped fuel a protest movement that was violent, but often limited to a generic anarchism that bypassed the unhappy experience of pure, blinkered economics. In art, similar condemnations can be found in the paintings of Shigeru Onishi, Jirō Yoshihara, Takashi Fukushima, and later the Gutai group.

Architects, at least initially, did not follow suit, being too preoccupied with the massive task of reconstruction. It was only

25 "In order to build up Japan as a base for the Korean War and as a bastion against communism, America flooded aid funds into the country. In the peak year of 1953, payment by the United Nations for services and supplies amounted to 594.6 million dollars and although the amount fell in the following years it was still some 320 million dollars in 1957. This as well as the large sums of US aid given to the Japanese to assist recovery (in 1947 alone the sum involved was about 400 million dollars) provided much-needed capital." Michael Edwardes, *Asia in the Balance* (Harmondsworth: Penguin, 1962), 149. Japan's political dependence on the United States, the main factor in the wholesale revival of capitalism, was—and still is—the major obstacle that the Japanese progressive forces had to confront. "On January 19, 1960," writes Giampaolo Calchi Novati, "the revised Security Treaty with the United States was signed, attenuating the more restrictive rules on Japanese independence but confirming the treaty's military character. In May the same year, anti-American and anti-government demonstrations threatened the institutions and led to the cancellation of President Eisenhower's visit to Japan. The protests ran out of steam immediately after the sacking of Prime Minister Kishi, who had been unpopular even with some of his own party members because of his strong-arm tactics. The treaty was approved by a majority, however, without the Socialists, thanks to a legal loophole." Giampaolo Calchi Novati, "Due anni di governo Ikeda in Giappone," *Comunità*, no. 102 (1962).

in 1950, however, after the allocation of fifteen billion yen of government funds for the reconstruction of eighty thousand subsidized homes, that we find the first mention of a building program. Given the huge problems created by the shortage of building materials, not to mention the state of the construction industry and the real-estate market, this program could hardly be described as successful. The Japanese would pay the price for piecemeal planning that was focused only on the worst-hit sectors and, as such, ineffectual.

The act on subsidized housing was an important step in Japanese building policy. Thanks to this law and two other legislative measures approved around the same time, 1950 was a memorable year in the history of Japanese architecture. The first of these measures was to institute a democratic system of local authorities which were tasked with devising their own building programs.[26] The second was the result of a thirty-year campaign by Japanese architects for legal recognition of their status, a two-part process with the Ministry of Construction conferring a first degree at the end of university studies, and the local authorities confirming the qualification after a period of practice. At the beginning of the 1950s, there was little interest in architecture among Japanese society at large—as we learn from Professor Satow's presentation to the UNESCO International Conference of Artists in Venice in 1952. His words give us a measure of the progress made by Japanese culture over the last decade.[27]

This period saw the realization of the first projects in the sector that was the worst hit, and the only one to be properly planned: housing. To assess the scale of the effort, we need to remember that in 1945 there was a shortage of over four million houses, but that number was cut in half by the time the program for temporary homes was completed in 1958.

---

26    The system of local governance created in 1888 was consolidated in 1947 by a law dividing local governments into two categories: "prefectures and cities" and "towns and villages."

27    Koike, *Contemporary Architecture of Japan,* 17.

The difficulties of devising a coherent system of planning were compounded by further obstacles of a more cultural nature: a lack of awareness of the need for a modern approach to urban planning that would bring together the individual programs, and the burden of traditional building techniques and types that were completely incompatible with the modern methods required to resolve the problem of mass housing.

Thus the main efforts in housing were focused on the provision of the seemingly mandatory detached house with garden. Architects like Kenji Hirose, Kiyoshi Seike, and Gonkurō Kume continued the work begun in the prewar period by Horiguchi and Yoshida, designing residential areas with houses made of prefabricated metal and concrete elements. Hirose, in particular, from 1953 on, designed more than thirty types of single-family homes that could be reproduced in industrial quantities.

Hirose's system of steel construction had the further advantage of being easy to assimilate because of its affinities with traditional timber technology, which explains his success both with the general public and with the architects, among them Isao Shibaoka, Kiyoshi Seike, and Masahiro Shiono, who adopted his methods. By contrast, the earliest reinforced concrete houses—for example, Takamasa Yoshizaka's Villa Coucou, where concrete is used with typical Corbusian brutality—sparked fierce debate in Japanese architectural circles. The need to implement the subsidized construction program led architects to adopt these more modern types of housing, even though they were inimical to the national culture and tradition. With this, the problem that had plagued the 1930s debate on modernity and tradition returned in amplified form.

The new development of society along the lines of industrial capitalism, the stabilization of middle-class democracy, and greater civil liberties—all these, inevitably, contributed to another historical crisis that resulted in an even more profound break with what remained of the feudal structures and traditions. Once more, this raised the question of a synthesis of the two contrasting worlds. And as happened after the Shogun was deposed, the need for such an accord arose from a violent rupture with the past, rather than from the process of self-creation of a society. And yet again the proposed synthesis was described as "westernization," a distortion of the peculiar characteristics that define the concept of "synthesis."

This time, however, the revival of capitalism, and all the inequalities it engendered, was met with the rise of a new governing class that was willing to fight against feudalism and impose its own system of rule—a more or less enlightened nationalistic middle-class despotism. But there was also a common will among the people, a response to the immense catastrophe of the atomic bomb and the unimaginable devastation it unleashed, which was as much social and cultural as it was physical. In face of the vast scale of destruction, the collective annihilation, the radical overturning of all established values, it could no longer be a question of establishing guidelines for reconstruction that were consistent with history, because history itself had been violated. The more vital elements in Japan engaged in merciless self-analysis, committed to seeking the underlying reasons for the war that had caused so much loss of life. They could not—given the tragic dimensions of the catastrophe that had befallen them—behave like the West German government, with its insensible display of indifference and agnosticism.

The different aspects characterizing recent Japanese history thus came into sharper relief. They became a contradiction, a vital contradiction: as society developed in a decidedly neo-capitalistic direction, oriented toward an indifferent consumer society, the livelier intellectual forces and the working class joined forces to fight against the spread of the "agnosticism of production" and "passivity of consumption."

Japanese culture displayed an extreme sensitivity—as we have already had occasion to note—toward these complex processes, responding to them in a more or less mature, critical way. The dissonances created by the introduction of new techniques that contrasted with traditional methods were absorbed. Initially, this response was conditioned by the state of mute stupor that followed the atomic tragedy, but then the contrast was accepted and the search for integration shifted to a higher cultural level. Charlotte Perriand, an astute observer of Japanese life, analyzed the consequences of modernization at a distance of some eleven years from the end of the war. Though sometimes superficial, her view of 1950s Japan is revealing:

> Tokyo 1956, modern buildings, small iron and concrete fortresses that contain surprising complexes one on top of the other: railway stations, subways, stores, restaurants, and theatres ...
> At their feet a paper-and-wood city of eight million inhabitants: seething, crude life, as in the Middle Ages ...
> This eruption of life is what makes Japan so seductive: festive urban quarters celebrating with ephemeral decorations of paper lanterns and garlands. These are the expression of a local neighborhood, of the individual inhabitants, of the whole population ...
> The Japanese are eager for new knowledge and are full of respect—perhaps even too respectful—for anything they either don't understand or only understand a little. Thrown headlong into the modern adventure, they find everything possible, everything conceivable—they take up all novelties, insatiable but alive ... Imagine returning to a Paris straight out of the Middle Ages, where all the ancient customs are conserved but the city is embellished with modern constructions. Do you realize what would be conjured up before our eyes?[28]

These vital aspects are thus inherent in the discontinuities, the fractures and the compromises, that the Japanese take as the basis of their new search for continuity.

"Moreover"—Perriand goes on—"Japan now depends on our world and to guarantee a living for its people ... production

---

28  Charlotte Perriand, "Crisi del gusto in Giappone," *Casabella continuità*, no. 210 (1957): 55–57.

is geared to satisfy the need for exports, which are different from its own needs and life experience, and this insidiously modifies the country's traditional character."[29]

It is interesting to note how European observers tended to highlight aspects of the new Japanese culture that had parallels in the context of the west. In all likelihood, they saw in its various motivating forces and contradictions a potential catalyst that would precipitate new solutions and suggest—principally to Europe—a way of addressing issues that were shared by cultures whose crises were becoming more and more alike.

Perriand's impressionistic images, however, fail to grasp the underlying political reality that helps to explain the contradictions she describes: the modernization of society was achieved at the cost of the rise to power of the class closest to the reactionary ideology of the Tojo regime. In effect, the Liberal Democratic Party, created in 1955 through the merging of the liberal and progressive parties, became the mouthpiece for the conservative policies of the large industrial monopolies, while the practice of political patronage, the connivance of the lesser authorities, and the first-past-the-post electoral system combined to guarantee the majority party a support base that was composite but extremely widespread, especially in rural areas.

The working-class parties, confined to the opposition, had very little influence during this period. But on the strength of a solid ideological platform, they forged alliances with students and intellectuals and vigorously fought against rearmament, defense pacts, and pro-American policies. The reactionary intransigence of expansionist capitalism would be countered by unwavering democratic opposition, and in this context recent architectural experiments have taken on a particular significance.

The architectural culture of the 1950s, however, did not immediately find working methods or tools that reflected the new conditions of a society in an increasing state of foment, and this undoubtedly contributed to the fragile connection of

---

29   Perriand, "Crisi del gusto in Giappone," 66.

the general public to the field of architecture and the urgent problems raised by the reconstruction.

Because of this, the vocabulary of international rationalism became a precise reference point for Japanese architecture in the immediate postwar period. The major buildings realized in the 1950s, with the exception of some pioneering works (discussed below), thus have a remarkably homogeneous functionalist appearance. Only occasionally do we see a conscious attempt at an aesthetic synthesis, although it must be acknowledged that these buildings are generally of a fairly high standard.

The pavilions built between 1949 and 1951 for Keio University in Tokyo,[30] for example, have a deliberately restrained expressiveness. The elements of the language are muted but calibrated in such a way as to achieve a synthesis that is not far removed from traditional solutions, and serves as a means of controlling the figuration. The same is true of the offices of Hideo Kosaka's Sendai Insurance Company (1951), and of more complex buildings such as the Kyoto Railway Station (1952) designed by the Kyoto City Engineering Department, or the Sumiyoshi Apartments in Osaka (1951) designed by the Showa Studio, which show signs of an attempt to define a new kind of residential organization.

In addition to this group of works, we can also consider other examples that address more interesting issues and are more individual in style, without going so far as to break with the cultural line summarized above. Raymond's works, in particular, were an important model in continuity with the prewar experience. His mature works, such as the Reader's Digest Headquarters in Tokyo (1951; fig. 20), the US Department of State Residential Apartments in Tokyo (1952; fig. 21), designed in collaboration with Ladislav Leland Rado, and the headquarters of the musical instrument company Nippon (1953), already reveal

30   Published in Koike, *Contemporary Architecture of Japan*, 81–86. We can, however, establish parallels between the deliberate restraint of this group of works and many other international projects in the immediate postwar period, due to a well-founded distrust in the ideological and figurative ideas of rationalism, which was then clearly on the wane although it was still found in new constructions.

Fig. 20 Antonin Raymond, Reader's Digest Headquarters, Tokyo

Fig. 21 Antonin Raymond, US Department of State Residential Apartments, Tokyo

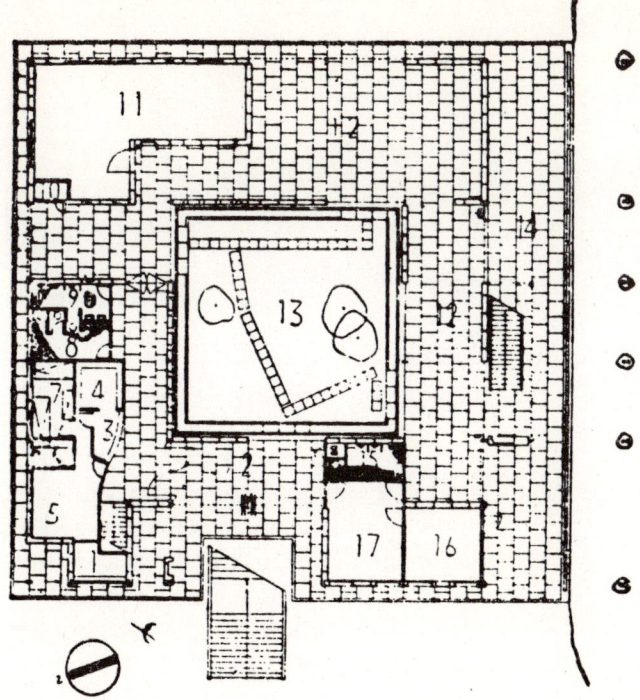

Fig. 22
Junzō Sakakura,
Museum of
Modern Art,
Kamakura, plan

the potential for integrating the vocabulary of the International Style with an interpretation of the local context, a development all the more significant as it was pursued by a foreign architect.

At the same time, there were some important new works by the pioneers of the Japanese modern movement. Murano's Takashimaya in Tokyo makes clear the line of continuity with his own work of the 1930s, while Sakakura's Museum of Modern Art in Kamakura (1951) is undoubtedly one of the finest buildings of those years, with a clarity of organization and a critical awareness of the figurative means deployed (figs. 22 and 23).

There are also some buildings by younger architects that show a desire for deeper experimentation that goes beyond acquired knowledge and takes nothing for granted. In 1952, the office of Kunio Maekawa won the competition for the

Fig. 23
Junzō Sakakura,
Museum of
Modern Art,
Kamakura

Kanagawa Prefectural Concert Hall and Library in Yokohama (fig. 24). Built in 1955, the design was mainly developed by a young architect in the team, Masato Ōtaka. After joining Maekawa at the end of the war, Ōtaka became one of his principal collaborators and a decisive influence on the direction of the practice. With its precise organization, based on a clear identification of the different functions of the library and auditorium, and its vigorous treatment of the surfaces and the exposed structural elements in the interior, the complex already marks a departure from the prevailing style of Japanese rationalism. Nonetheless, it remains a study, a test of the validity of a somewhat reduced means of expression.

In 1953, Maekawa completed the construction of the Nippon Sōgo Bank in Tokyo (fig. 25). Here, the pure stereometric volumes and canonical ribbon windows are combined with a dynamic approach to the basement and attic zones, in which an interplay of recesses and projections foreshadows later developments in Maekawa's poetics, albeit in a way that is still too slavishly dependent on the repertoire of 1930s rationalism.

But despite their intrinsic interest and their prefiguring of contemporary motifs, these works only represent the second phase of Japanese architecture's journey toward a practical methodology rooted in the real requirements of a country rapidly undergoing dramatic change.

This second phase followed a initial phase in which the passive acceptance of imported methods gave way to a more

Fig. 24
Kunio Maekawa,
Kanagawa
Prefectural
Concert Hall
and Library,
Yokohama

Fig. 25
Kunio Maekawa,
Sōgo Bank,
Tokyo

POSTWAR ARCHITECTURE

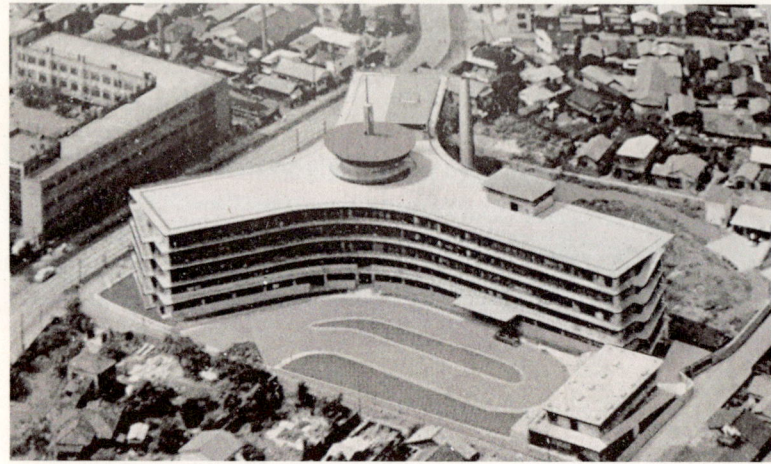

Fig. 26
Mamoru
Yamada,
Teishin
Hospital,
Tokyo

Fig. 27
Hiroshi Ōe,
Hōsei University,
Tokyo

thoughtful, but not yet original, interpretation of a repertoire and a synthesis, applied flexibly to all manner of programs, to explore the full range of possibilities.

A number of buildings of a high standard were realized in this phase. One of these is Mamoru Yamada's Teishin Hospital in Tokyo (1953), with its Y-shaped plan centered around a spiral ramp that provides access for ambulances: however, the building lacks an autonomous figurative rationale, remaining bound to a blatantly functionalist schema (fig. 26). Hiroshi Ōe's Hōsei University (1955–58), on the other hand, is arguably the most significant construction of the 1950s. Its clear-cut volumetric organization and well-proportioned curtain wall facades have an expressive neutrality which appears strangely in contrast with the violent destruction visited on the country (fig. 27).

With a few exceptions, this neutrality would define the buildings constructed in the late 1950s. It was as if architects had needed to pause for reflection, to suspend judgment for a while, before they could gain a full understanding of the reality of the situation and achieve a conscious, mature means of critical expression. In this period of transition, the study of function seemed the most suitable response to the urgent needs of the country, to the point where it consumed almost all the interest of the project.

## 2. Kenzō Tange's early works

It was against this backdrop that Kenzō Tange completed the Hiroshima Peace Memorial Park (figs. 28–30). A former assistant of Maekawa, Tange had already designed several works, including his own house in the Setagaya district of Tokyo, a clear (and controversial) attempt to fuse modern architecture and Japanese tradition. Elements of that tradition persist in the use of opaque and translucent panels and in the overall organization of the interior, even if the classic module of the tatami mat (0.99 x 1.98m) was replaced by measurements based on Le Corbusier's Modulor.

But it was the Hiroshima Peace Memorial Park that brought Tange international fame, and the work assumed a vital importance in the history of modern architecture in Japan, not just for its aesthetic qualities, but as a marker of a turning point in the Japanese architecture scene of the 1950s.[31]

It would not be correct, however, to see the Peace Memorial Park solely in terms of a radical departure, for it is also an example of continuity with the cultural development of the Japanese rationalist movement. We see a preoccupation with critically exploring the tenets of rationalism by clarifying its methodology—testing how far it was possible to push its limits, so to speak. This critical exploration led Tange to go beyond the initial scope of his research.

Tange won the commission as the result of an international competition in 1946.[32] The construction had to be inserted into

---

31    Some western observers also pointed this out when the work was first published. See, for example, V. G., "Il centro della Pace ad Hiroshima," *Casabella continuità*, no. 212 (1956): 14.
32    The first prize was not awarded, so Tange was given the commission as runner up. The construction was widely covered in the first issue of the international edition of the magazine *Shinkenchiku* (1956). The spiritual value of the Memorial Park was stressed by Tange himself: "There are two views of Hiroshima. Some think that the project should not be built while there are still homeless people; others believe that the two types of reconstruction can proceed in parallel. We are convinced that the special situation of Hiroshima, which concerns the whole world, justifies the construction of this Peace Project at the same time as the housing program." K. Tange, "Giappone, Hiroshima, un nuovo centro di ricreazione," in *CIAM: Il cuore della città*, ed. E. N. Rogers, J. L. Sert, and J. Tyrwhitt (Milan: Hoepli, 1954), 137.

Fig. 28
Kenzō Tange,
Hiroshima
Peace Memorial
Park

POSTWAR ARCHITECTURE

Fig. 29
Kenzō Tange,
Hiroshima Peace
Memorial Park

Fig. 30
Kenzō Tange,
Hiroshima Peace
Memorial Park

an appalling patchwork of vast open fields levelled by the bomb and new areas hastily built with few resources. In the national narrative (and indeed in world history) the name Hiroshima had come to stand for the tragic epilogue to World War II, but for the Japanese people this epilogue had a further specific meaning, marking the beginning of new, more democratic chapter in their history.

In this respect the program for the Memorial Park was significant: a civic center, a pavilion for exhibitions, a museum, and a commemorative monument (Memorial Cenotaph). A series of buildings for life, for social contact, as a homage to the war dead and, moreover, a warning for future generations.

Tange was extremely punctilious in following the brief. It was not the moment—even if the size of the complex would have allowed it—to indulge in flights of expression that might easily have degenerated into evasiveness. The whole focus was on the future, but rather than facile, gratuitous optimism there was an explicit declaration of belief, a pledge. Tange's buildings are made of exposed reinforced concrete and raised from the ground on a system of *pilotis*, bringing to mind the essential expressiveness and rigor of Corbusian architecture. But at the same time, there are more or less explicit references to traditional architecture in the form of some of the structural elements and the proportions and modulations of the infills. The result is a vision of the future that re-examines the past and its historical value. This vision becomes even clearer, in architectural terms, in the reinforced concrete monument that is set apart from the three main aligned buildings. It is also worth noting the hieratic nature of this arrangement. The curving plasticity of the cenotaph is reminiscent of the prehistoric form of the Japanese house, as shown in some models in archaeological museums. Past and future touch, and this dialectic between the expressive form of the monument and the dry, contained, lean essentiality of the exhibition pavilion, museum, and civic center is perhaps the most potent aspect of Tange's design.

With the Hiroshima Peace Memorial Park, Japan seemed to speak a precise and personalized language for the first time. A deeper analysis reveals that the elements of that language are derived from multiple sources in the international style, and what is new in the design is the way the elements are organized and the spirit with which they are applied and shaped. Moreover, in the Memorial Park, Japan's adoption of modernism—meditated but initially not mature—now becomes a recognition of the correlation between two traditions, between Japanese and modern architecture. Tange gives a practical demonstration of a new synthesis that goes beyond the sterile debates on the need (or not) for a "national way" of adhering to the modern movement.

One could also note the degree of maturity with which this experiment is conducted, particularly in relation to the series of failed attempts in Italian architecture (but the same applies to many countries in Europe and America), in which the ideas of historical authenticity and "tradition" have degenerated into exercises in populism or deplorable escapism.

The arrival of Tange's park marked a radical turning point in an architectural scene that had been of a fairly high standard but rather directionless. Immediately it sparked a series of heated debates that had the merit of stimulating a critical re-examination of the country's architectural culture, as can be read directly in the experiences of those years.

## 3. Mature rationalism (1953–57)

From 1953 to 1957, a series of new buildings raised—albeit in a different way and with varying degrees of success—the same issues that were highlighted in the analysis of Tange's key, symptomatic work. One such project is the International House (1955) in Tokyo, the outcome of a collaboration between Maekawa, Sakae, and Yoshimura (fig. 31). The three architects had similar apprenticeships: Maekawa and Sakae had worked in Le Corbusier's atelier before the war, while Yoshimura, along with Maekawa, had collaborated with Raymond.

The organization of the building, which was used for international cultural exchanges, is based on a clear division of the plan into counterposed blocks, an explicit evocation of the dialectically linked volumes of historic Japanese buildings. This reference, moreover, is echoed in the use of typical elements and modulations from traditional architecture, which are then inserted into an unequivocally modern context, clearly derived from Le Corbusier. The extent to which these historical memories remain evident in the work—on purpose, of course—is determined by an effective, authentic integration of the two traditions which strengthens and makes explicit their common denominator.

If the International House fails to reach the expressive heights and distinctiveness of Tange's contemporaneous Tokyo City Hall (also known as Tokyo Metropolitan Government Building), it makes an important contribution as a vivid demonstration that the issue at stake went far beyond a simple question of style.

In this third stage of experimentation, Japanese architects deployed linguistic elements that were by now part of the tradition of the modern movement and adopted modes of organization that were explicitly linked to "rationalist" culture in the strictest sense. However, the rigidity and evident limitations of the works we have looked at so far suggest that the new set of problems called for a new approach to the figurative aspect of architecture, a new way of using the means of expression that would highlight and make more explicit the ideas that were

Fig. 31
Kunio Maekawa, International House, Tokyo

now being consciously formulated. The language of rationalism offered a powerful advantage in this regard: it created a shared platform which allowed an effective exchange of experience in a movement that was collective in several ways. The initial experiments were taken up and developed further within this shared platform, which for the Japanese modern movement already had a distinctive character, representing a continuity and a legacy to be safeguarded.

This was the direction that Tange had already taken in the Tokyo City Hall (1952–55), though the building was completed too late to have much impact on the internal architectural culture. Other projects of the time attempted to renew the language of Japanese architecture following paths that were markedly different from the ones indicated by the works of Tange and Maekawa.

Among the most noteworthy attempts are the works of Hiroshi Ōe (see the Hōsei University above), who pursued a refined rarefaction of the vocabulary of rationalism, reducing it to elementary geometric and structural forms that have an essential, archaic quality which is not so removed from traditional models. In the Miki Building in Tokyo (fig. 32), the expressive emphasis of the structural framework, pushed to the point of

Fig. 32
Hiroshi Ōe,
Miki Building,
Tokyo

Fig. 33
Yoshinobu
Ashihara, Chuo
Koron Building

abstraction, endows the building with a dream-like quality that contrasts strangely with the semantic content that the same elements usually have in international style architecture. Here we find a kind of translation into Japanese of the most rigorous rationalist syntax, in which the initial "constructivist" motifs gain an expressiveness through a process of refinement and rarefaction—a powerful process of critical thinking. That critical thinking, however, fails to go beyond the limits imposed by the syntax, and consequently only acts on the syntax from within.

Some very similar buildings were designed by Yoshinobu Ashihara on his return to Japan from the United States, where he had studied with Marcel Breuer.[33] His first work, the Chuo Koron Building (fig. 33), updates through the treatment of individual details or the texture of materials an otherwise slightly revivalist approach that emphasizes and meticulously reiterates the principles of rationalism. Ashihara does not reach the same heights of refinement as Ōe—his explorations of the language lack the same critical content—nor does he achieve the kind of

---

33   Ashihara worked in Junzō Sakakura's practice in 1946–47 before taking up a Fulbright scholarship to the US, where he studied at Yale and Harvard.

POSTWAR ARCHITECTURE

Fig. 34 Yoshinobu Ashihara, Yokohama Women's Cultural Center

almost ironic abstraction we see in the Miki Building. Surer in his convictions, he wants to explore the full potential of rationalism. Thus, the rigorous form of the Matsuhama Clubhouse in Niigata (1957) is given an allusive incline, whereas the Yokohama Women's Cultural Center (fig. 34) injects a certain energy into the formulas of the International Style. This last building can be seen as emblematic of a particular approach in Japanese architecture: without achieving the distinctiveness of the works of Tange or Maekawa, it re-elaborates and combines repertoires and syntaxes from various sources, achieving a synthesis that is vaguely eclectic but not inexpressive.

Other works by Ashihara are more controlled but less effective overall, with the rationalist approach verging on a rather unwieldy purism. Thus, the Nikko Hotel in downtown Tokyo, a steel construction, has vaguely Miesian overtones, while the Seaside Youth Club and Yokohama Civic Hospital speak of an attempt to achieve a more complex articulation without ever straying too far from the International Style. If these reaffirmations of the validity of rationalist poetics often yielded notable results, their influence on the development of Japanese architecture was limited, soon overtaken by the astonishing momentum of the new approach developed by the youngest generations along with some of the "masters." Unsurprisingly, this style has attracted growing international interest.

Fig. 35
Junzō Sakakura,
Tokyo-Kaikan
Building

1954 saw the completion of Sakakura's Tokyu-Kaikan Building, commissioned by the Ministry of Transport in cooperation with a commercial company whose retail premises extend over a large part of the site (fig. 35).[34] More than the intrinsic features of the architecture, what is interesting is the new approach to tackling the major problems of a metropolis like Tokyo. The Tokyu-Kaikan Building is located not far from the hub of Shibuya, at the heart of city, where the main lines of communication that link the Japanese capital to the rest of the country converge: one million people pass through here every day, transported by several main railway lines, the metro, the regional subway, buses, and trams. Sakakura's project restructures the whole square, providing a large multipurpose building to cater for the huge numbers converging on the interchange, a bus station, an elevated highway with associated parking lots, and a cultural center. It creates an urban nucleus in an area already equipped with major transport infrastructure.

The Tokyu-Kaikan Building can be seen as the earliest example of a new approach to the pressing issues facing contemporary architecture and as a prelude to further experimentation. We will now look at two buildings that are already in some ways the mature expression of that new direction.

34   See the details of the project in *Architecture d'aujourd'hui*, no. 65 (1956): 87–91.

## 4. The first results of the new direction: Tokyo City Hall and the Sogō Department Store

Two buildings completed almost simultaneously in 1957 in the heart of Tokyo, again alongside a major transport hub, represent a key development in the history of Japanese modern architecture, each contributing to its culture in different ways.

Tange's new City Hall and Murano's Sogō Department Store were a great success with Tokyoites, who had previously demonstrated only a lukewarm interest in modern architecture. In fact, the public could hardly avoid expressing an opinion about a pair of buildings that play such an important functional role in the city: one of them the seat of the city government, the other a commercial center, characterized as usual by Murano's interest in social issues. However, the pair are also significant from the point of view of the cityscape: standing side by side, the two large buildings gave the Japanese capital a completely new look.

Thus, almost by chance—the siting of the buildings was not determined by a unitary urban plan with clearly defined objectives—the inhabitants of Tokyo were suddenly confronted with the physical dimension and expressive dimension of a revolutionary architecture that ruptured the traditional fabric and space of the city. The completion of the buildings can be seen as marking the end of a transitional period for modern architecture in Japan—a period in which the best part of its energy was focused on defining a specific role for the country within the development of the international modern movement.

With Tange's City Hall and Murano's department store, one chapter ended and a new one began. The exploration of methodologies and repertoires drawn from international sources came to a close, along with the frantic experimentalism that had dominated the years from 1953 to 1957. The new chapter, still ongoing, has seen the flourishing of themes and buildings that have attracted so much international interest in Japanese architecture. Tange's City Hall can be seen as a bridge toward these radical new developments (even though the project was

Fig. 36
Kenzō Tange,
Tokyo City
Hall, model
view

begun as early as 1953, the year he won the competition organized by the Tokyo Metropolitan Administration).

Traces of the severity typical of Tange's early works, in particular the Hiroshima Peace Memorial Park, can still be seen in the City Hall, both in its schematic organization (fig. 36)—its mechanical juxtaposition of the elongated office block and the volume of the council chambers—and in the rigidity and concision of its details, structure, facade modulation (figs. 37 and 38). However, the way the various elements are organized and integrated into an overall unity already speaks of a different approach, a new spirit. Within the same clearly defined mass, two different zones—a basement zone directly connected to the grounds, the street, and the pedestrian area, and a raised zone that underscores the urban function of the building—are counterposed and unified by the insistent repetition of the module of the loggia, which is then taken up, and tempered by, the dark shaded areas at the base of the complex and the arrangement of the external ramps (fig. 39).

These figurative dialectics reveal Tange's polemical attitude to the more or less orthodox functionalism that had taken hold throughout Japan. Tange's statements—"space precedes

Fig. 37
Kenzō Tange,
Tokyo City Hall

Fig. 38
Kenzō Tange,
Tokyo City Hall

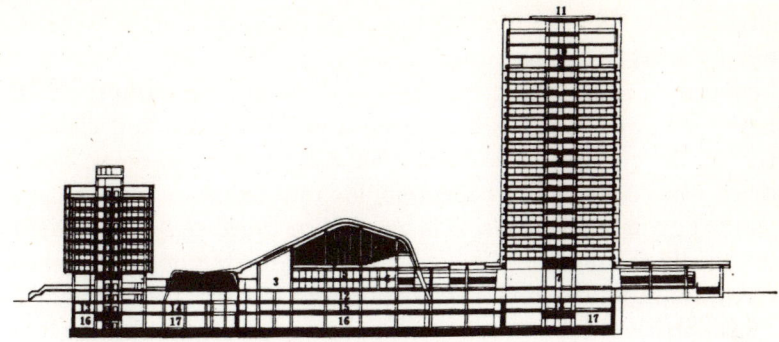

Fig. 39
Kenzō Tange,
Tokyo City
Hall, section

function" or "only beautiful things are functional"—might be considered ingenuous from a rigorously critical point of view. In his practical translation of those concepts, however, he displays an exceptional maturity, carefully avoiding any kind of wishful thinking or fancifulness. The close bond between the configuration of the complex and its civic program is, moreover, stressed by Tange himself in his criticism of the way the typical city hall in the US had been reduced to little more than an anonymous bureaucratic shell:

> On the contrary, we feel that the city hall must be restored to its original role of inviting the population to join in common purpose. This tradition never existed in Japan, where similar buildings represented only the ruling power. As architects, we wish to help the population achieve this consciousness by making the municipal complex the 'spiritual center' of our capital. Consequently, the scale of the entrance hall is welcoming, rather than monumental; likewise, the mezzanine-level pedestrian route that joins the city to the building responds to the same psychological need to invite people to gather round the symbol of their city.[35]

35   Kenzō Tange, "La Municipalité de Tokyo," *Architecture d'aujourd'hui*, no. 82 (1959): 89.

The plastic form of the volume containing the council chambers, placed as a mediating element—in reality, a focal point—between the administrative block and the (as yet unbuilt) office tower takes on a symbolic meaning as the figure that characterizes the complex as a whole. We will consider in more detail below the consistency of the complex in relation to Tange's later work. For now, however, it is enough to point out the element of "gridlock" in the Tokyo City Hall: namely, the problem of recovering the "communicative" values of the architectural image through the direct insertion of an expressive form into the body of the city on the one hand, and an iniquitous political and social situation on the other.

The need to recover the "semantic power of the image" has in recent years been a crucial theme not only in the international debate but in a series of developments within Japanese modern culture. Having achieved an independent level of maturity, that culture has been able to look to its own history and traditions for methods and precedents that offer alternatives or solutions to problems that the European and American modern movements have been struggling to resolve.

Once again, we see the need for a synthesis achieved through the "contradictory unity of cultures." For the Japanese, this has meant infusing the "elective affinity" between modernism and traditional Japanese architecture with a new independent and progressive content. (In relation to this, Tange's statements on the importance of the Imperial Palace of Kyoto as the *ideal* reference for design of the City Hall seem quite revealing.[36])

Although Murano's approach to the configuration of the Sogō Department Store differs in many ways from that of the adjacent building by Tange, there is an affinity in terms of its problematics and its rationale that is far from coincidental (fig. 40).

36    "During the competition I reconsidered the Imperial Palace of Kyoto with its huge cornices, roofs and cypress-bark coverings, its pillars and broad verandahs ... I wouldn't go so far as to say there was a direct relation between the Imperial Palace and the Tokyo City Hall, but simply that the harmony and equilibrium of the palace informed my spirit while I was designing." Tange, "Giappone, Hiroshima," 92.

Fig. 40
Tōgō Murano, Sogō Department Store, Tokyo

Fig. 41
Tōgō Murano, Sogō Department Store, Tokyo, interior

Firstly, the "dimension" of the building: the word is in quote marks because it is used here to indicate not a physical quantity—one that is in any case imposed by the brief—but rather a figurative quality that is intrinsic to the form of the building and that goes beyond the traditional approach to the relation between building and city.

In this new relationship, we can readily see a clear element of continuity with Murano's own prewar architecture, such as the Department Store that he built for the same company in Osaka in 1935. And this continuity extends beyond the figurative aspect to encompass the planning of the building, which is again conceived as a center of social exchange (fig. 41), and in this sense its proximity to the City Hall becomes even more important.

For Murano this continuity of experience is to be found in the continual renewal of his means of expression—a renewal that is driven, not by formal schemas, but by a highly distinctive methodology and aesthetic intent.

The triangular configuration of the site determines the plan of the Sogō Department Store in Tokyo, which appears as a single volume, massive but compact, its concise character vigorously delineated. Here, the details play a dialectical role in the overall volumetric organization: the continuity of the surfaces (the true protagonist of Murano's architecture) is powerfully stated by the dense horizontal concrete-framed glass blocks of the external walls, and interrupted only by a few small apertures and by the narrow linear gap that separates the upper part of the building from the volume below, emphasizing the striking plasticity of the external cladding.

Even elements that might be considered incidental in relation to the overall form have been absorbed in a balanced composition and exploited for their figurative potential: the publicity signs, for example, through their design and positioning, both respond to and highlight the concision of the body of the building, which makes no concessions to "current" taste in architectural forms.

But despite the coherence and originality of the design, this work has what might be called, at a stretch, an *academic* character; Murano's preoccupation with completeness and figurative harmony has given it the feel of a building that is entirely closed out, or at least that allows little room for interpretive freedom.

Murano's department stores are the highest expressions of an architectural culture that systematically developed the rationalist methodology of the 1930s; in the works of this Japanese master we see a vital response to the new demands of the time. Ultimately, however, it is in Tange's City Hall that we see the mature embodiment of what might be described as the "new school" of Japanese architecture.

## 5. The new school of Japanese architecture

Before analyzing the works of this new school, it is necessary to attempt a broader interpretation of the phenomenon that Russell Bourne has called the "architectural renaissance" in Japan. This will also provide an opportunity to sum up the story so far.

The new research undertaken by Tange, Maekawa, Sakakura, taka, and some younger architects is concerned with one of the crucial problems in today's international debate, which is referred to in some quarters as the "crisis of constructivism." Constructivism is used here not to denote a style, but to describe the autonomous and decisive contribution of artistic activity to the development of political and social structures, as conceived by twentieth-century avant-gardes. This conception of art, which encompasses a way of being, a way of formulating the role of culture and of the intellectual, laid the basis for the artistic revolution in our century, but today it needs to be totally reassessed.

The crisis of rationalism was initially felt less in Japan than elsewhere, given the historical conditions of the country. Already apparent in the immediate aftermath of World War II, it spoke of the need for a profound renewal of both the language of rationalism and its methodologies. Japanese architects may have been late to realize the extent of the crisis, but they responded with some remarkable solutions displaying a common purpose that is perhaps unique in the current panorama of the modern movement.

What were—still are—the factors in this crisis? The constructivism of art was called into question: the constructivism that had been invoked in the 1930s as means to act on the very structure of society, to reshape it through the modification of production. Fascist ideologues around the world—including in Japan—were among the fiercest critics of this constructivism, but also its best interpreters, fully recognizing its deep ethical strength as a dangerous obstacle that had to be crushed if they were to impose their dictatorships. By the end of the war, the time for illusions was past. Gradually the major missteps gave way to a greater maturity that heralded new concerns and new dimensions for the work of the architect and the artist.

That work was no longer about defining, through the construction of space, a precise methodology for living, or about embracing an ideal rationalist principle that would bring together theory and practice, artistic and critical processes. Nor did it propose to redeem the human condition or to remedy unjust relations of production through improvements to production techniques.

Now, instead, rationalism was called on to provide a reservoir of constant forms that had the capacity to identify and meet the ever-changing needs of modern life (while at the same time safeguarding some bourgeois values). The integration of technology and the creative act became a means of quantifying a quality that was to be preserved as the *ultima ratio* in a world that was losing sight of historical values—and also a means to go beyond class conflict. In Japan, however, these key tenets of the heroic age of modernism did not find the historical ground or cultural substrate they needed to latch onto: at least not in their original form.

I deliberately omitted one observation from my assessment of the work of Japanese architects in the 1930s, holding it in reserve for this description of the overall historical situation. It is that these early projects are noteworthy for their figurative interpretations of the language of international architecture, but in terms of their overt ideological aims they are only tenuously linked to the Deutscher Werkbund or the Bauhaus.

The Werkbund first, and then the Bauhaus, systematically developed a theory of art that ignored *nature*, or rather proposed itself as an alternative to nature. Combining theory with practice, they sought to construct a *new nature*, one that was based on industry and extended the constructive process to the whole of society, which would become in this way self-managing, "identifying, in turn, with that production as a producer and user."[37] From today's perspective we can see clearly how this great illusion was conjured by intellectuals in the face of the impending social revolution and the collapse of the myths and traditions that had shaped their culture. An episode in the "revolution of technocrats" that aimed to salvage the original core of that culture, the illusion was an attempt to mediate between the new demands raised by the working classes and the ideal construction of the bourgeois world: the promotion of quality was precisely a program for the redistribution of the experience of art, previously a privilege reserved for only one segment of society. The same capitalist bourgeoisie responded to that generous illusion with a reappraisal of the myths of blood and barbarism. The modern movement was then faced with the dilemma of whether to retreat from its own positions or to form alliances with the more enlightened and ever more powerful capitalists who were pursuing their own reform agendas in an increasingly coherent way.

In the immediate postwar period, Japanese artists and architects were generally not ready to respond to the complex questions raised by European modernism: their own conditions of struggle distanced them somewhat from the situation in Europe. In Japan, the rise to power of the capitalist bourgeoisie was a relatively recent phenomenon. If the social revolution of the nineteenth century was closely tied to the development of capitalism, there was little in the way of an accompanying intellectual tradition to nourish the illusion of the revolutionary potential of the absolute autonomy of culture—at least in the meaning attributed to autonomy in the 1930s. Instead, the socio-economic conditions illustrated all too clearly the eminently autocratic character of the industrial revolution. In Japan, too, it was the role of the bourgeoisie to demolish any possible illusions.

For this reason, prewar Japanese architecture cannot be described as *ideological* in the same way that European architecture was. The absence in Japan of an equivalent to the theory of the "cell" and the "series"—the prime elements of the *Existenzminimum*, the ideological cornerstone of experimentation in *Mitteleuropa*—is not simply attributable to the fact that the

---

37   Giulio C. Argan, *Walter Gropius e la Bauhaus* (Turin: Einaudi, 1951), 38.

industry was less developed. Likewise, Japanese architects did not attempt to go beyond naturalism and intellectualism, as the programs of the Werkbund and Bauhaus did: these issues did not take root in Japanese society, or fuel new social demands. Rather, the naturalism found in much Japanese architecture was a means of reviving values that were overlooked by European culture but still valid in the eastern world: through naturalism, it was possible to recuperate the symbolic values that were ostensibly alien to the modern movement.

Integrating the importance of symbols and of the imagination with the issues of large-scale construction, involving repetition, standardization, and industrialization, constituted a way of overcoming the schematic nature of European rationalism—the fundamental problem that constructivists had failed to address in their architecture, even though they were fond of raising it in their theoretical presuppositions and studies. But it should be noted that the history of Japanese architecture reveals a long tradition—one that is still considered valid—of establishing types and repetition based on standard elements. Thus the effort to integrate two quite distant traditions that we see as the starting point (or end result, depending on the case) of the most interesting and mature work by Japanese architects in the 1930s seems to have been guided—not entirely consciously, but more instinctively—by a continuity of experience. In the postwar period, this effort would coalesce in the unified approach of the "new school," who took the tentative blending of forms from the eastern tradition and the modern movement one stage further, to create a realistic integration of cultures.

The search for a unified approach to experimentation almost led to a *new mannerism*, in the best sense of the term. But mannerism, again, is a phenomenon historically rooted in eastern culture. In Japan, it has a very different meaning than it has in Europe, which does not have the same artistic tradition of *selecting within continuity*. Understood in this way, mannerism became a means to endow standard solutions with a rich symbolic quality—not as an exercise in itself, but as part of search for a new approach to practice. At this point, the figurative definitions and contents of that search came into play. The response was a critical reconnection with the most recent works of Le Corbusier. But what was meant by this reproposing of Corbusian language, this uninhibited embrace of the manner of the French master?

The answer is certainly complex. Though largely unified, the movement has not had access to the same decisive "opportunity" that gave an ostensibly similar phenomenon in Brazil a substantially different outcome. With Maekawa and Sakakura we can see, from their very first works, the influence of the time they spent in Le Corbusier's rue de Sevres atelier, but it is also true that this influence has been manifested only sporadically, and almost exclusively at a figurative level (in the narrowest sense of the word).

If we look, however, at the influence of Le Corbusier in countries like Brazil, North Africa, India, or Israel, we can frame the issue in a much wider context that can help us to understand the Japanese phenomenon in terms of its relations with international culture.

In all of these countries—Japan included—the European tradition became part of the national culture in various ways, either imposed through colonial domination, or absorbed through some contingent circumstance. Either way, adopting European tradition meant breaking with a culture that had for centuries been outside the orbit of the rationalistic, scientific civilization of the Mediterranean. Rationalism was taken up by these countries as an instrument for progress—in reality, it cut the ties to deep-rooted historical practices (as we already saw with the Meiji revolution in Japan). The fascination with Le Corbusier was based on the perception of his poetics: outside Europe, architects saw him not only as an heir to the great Enlightenment tradition but as an interpreter of the eastern symbolist tradition. More coherently than anyone else, Le Corbusier sought a *quality within the standard*, and looked to recover an image of architecture that was replete with meaning.[38]

Embracing the ideas that inform Le Corbusier's work was a way for the new school to position themselves in relation to many of the issues that were to feature in the international debate. It allowed them to continually broaden the scope of their work, for in eastern culture it is always important, if not essential, to choose a point of reference that becomes an ideal model, a basis for further exploration that can be successively refined: "We need to bear in mind," writes the German critic Udo Kultermann, "that for centuries the originality of an invention was of no importance in Japan, and the sole interest lay in the execution of the work, which acquired distinctive features through imperceptible nuances."[39] Like Benevolo, Kultermann discerns parallels with the crafts of medieval Europe.[40]

On the other hand, the young Japanese architects had no intention of reviving Le Corbusier's methodology, which always seeks to reduce problems to their basic terms. The French master's approach is diametrically opposed to the Japanese tradition of modulating a given element, composing infinite variations on a theme. But conversely that tradition may explain the lack of inhibition among Japanese architects about adopting a shared "mannerism"—a mannerism that is prodigious both in its quality and quantity.

For the new school, the brutalism of Le Corbusier's late works represents a central theme, but also a limit—go beyond it, and you risk wrecking, without any hope of salvage, the entire methodology of the modern movement. Their work combines an attitude of protest, undoubtedly also a lively component of Le Corbusier's late style, and an admonition—a tirade of ideas that attempt to point the way toward a new reality and foreshadow new ways of living.

38   On this subject, it can be argued that for Japanese architectural culture, Le Corbusier's work had a role as a benchmark and for historicization very similar to that exercised by eastern culture over European artists in the nineteenth century and early years of the twentieth century. Their respective positions were thus inverted in just under a century.
39   Udo Kultermann, *Architecture nouvelle au Japon* (Paris: Morancé, 1960), 11.
40   Benevolo, *History of Modern Architecture*, vol. 2, 774.

The elaboration of the working tools and language of architecture went hand in hand, therefore, with the elaboration of theories in which the more engaged architects explored the reasons for the contradictions that bedeviled the country in its advanced state of development. Out of this grew an almost spontaneous element of protest in architectural circles that was aligned with, but came after, parallel experiences in the fields of literature, painting, and cinema.[41] But equally, Japanese architects faced a specific task that remained urgent and could not be adequately addressed with generic professions of faith or incipient protests: whether they wanted to or not, they were directly involved in the construction of reality, in the widest possible sense of the term.

And so the distinctly autobiographical language of Le Corbusier's late works—a difficult, personal, potent language that was no longer concerned with providing repeatable models, but focused on the fraught dignity of the symbol and the monument—became the reference point for Japanese explorations, scaled up, produced in large quantities and subject to continuous verification.

But this remarkable operation had several intrinsic limits, which we will try to illuminate in the following analysis of the architecture of the new school, which will consider in detail the works of its three leading exponents: Tange, Maekawa, and Sakakura.

---

41  We are referring in particular to the expressionism of the abovementioned Shin-hanga art group, the film movement called Nakanai Realism (Realism Without Tears) and the new avant-garde painters whose "reviving through rupture" was very close to brutalism in architecture. "Going to the source of the fecund tradition to work within the international avant-garde", writes critic Tore Haga, "these two opposites meet to form a continuous circle among the Japanese elites, and artists such as the Gutai group, Domoto, or Sōfu Teshigahara. We have seen the dialectics that they use today with one of the richest Japanese traditions: the Zen tradition. Introduced into the spiritual world of the country in the twelfth century, this austere discipline of inner negation has opened up 'another' system in the thought and art of the Japanese and at the same time has released a deaf volcano of paroxysms in our souls. Zen philosophy has arguably rekindled the creative fire of the international avant-garde." Michel Tapié and Tore Haga, *Continuité et avant-garde au Japon* (Turin: Fratelli Pozzo, 1961).

## 6. Kenzō Tange

Tange's first internationally renowned works—as we have already established—represented a decisive break with tradition and with the rationalist mannerism of the immediate postwar period. In Japanese architectural culture, Tange is undoubtedly a unique, highly inspiring figure.

Of course, there are criticisms to be made, of his working methods, for example, which are in continuous ferment, and at times so preoccupied with achieving new forms of expression—so driven by nervous tension—that they neglect the necessary critical thinking and risk diluting the work. One could also point to the all-pervasive formalism of his research. But none of this criticism undermines the exceptional importance of his teaching, which confronts, head on, the break with the past. As Tange observes:

> The realities of present-day Japan, while part of historically conditioned worldwide reality, are at the same time given their unique shape by the traditions of Japan. Living within this reality, yet also trying always to comprehend it afresh in a forward-looking spirit, these traditions force themselves insistently upon our attention. Moreover, if the problems were not so urgent, we could quietly accept tradition almost unthinkingly as a hereditary custom or something outside of history. Only those with a forward-looking attitude realize that tradition exists and is alive. It is therefore only they who can confront and overcome it. This means neither elaborating grandiose schemes for the future nor being fatefully involved with the past, but awareness that the most vital task for today is creativity to elevate both past and future.[42]

---

42   Kenzō Tange, "Creation in Present-day Architecture and the Japanese Architectural Tradition," *Shinkenchiku*, June 1956: 25–33.

Fig. 42
Kenzō Tange,
Shimizu Town
Hall

While the Hiroshima Peace Memorial Park and the Tokyo City Hall were under construction, Tange completed some other buildings that are less innovative but still very interesting. Shimizu Town Hall (fig. 42), from 1954, provided the initial model for an administrative building that was to reach its finest expression in the Kagawa Prefectural Government Office on the island of Shikoku. At Shimizu, in fact, we already see the subdivision of the program into two distinct blocks: a lower block for offices dealing directly with the public, and a tower block accessible only to government workers.

Tange's adherence to the International Style is clear in the Shimizu Town Hall, and still legible in other minor works, such as the Tosho Printing Company Haramachi Factory at Numaza (1955; fig. 43) or the Tsuda College Library, Tokyo (1954), where he nonetheless finds a way to underline, time and again, the expressive potential of the structure, the repetition of the modular components, and the essential nature of the massing, always emphasizing the elements that relate to a synthesis of the various parts of the building as whole.

Fig. 43
Kenzō Tange,
Tosho Printing
Company
Haramachi
Factory

Thus, in the Children's Library that was added at a later stage to the Hiroshima Peace Memorial Park (fig. 44), the unique mushroom-shaped structure around which the interior space unfolds does not have the character of an architectural tour de force, but rather has a clean-cut simplicity and immediacy that gives it a special poetic quality.

In turn, the Kagawa Prefectural Government Office (figs. 45 and 46), completed in 1958, picks up the exploration Tange had begun in the Tokyo City Hall, searching for a way to integrate language of modernism and the traditional repertoire. Tange writes:

> In planning the Kagawa Prefectural Office, we purposefully considered separating the welfare facilities from other functions and placing them where the office workers could easily make use of them. We centered all welfare facilities on the fourth floor of the main building (this floor opens out on the roof of the lower block so good use can be made of the roof) making the whole story into a sort of recreation floor.[43]

[43] Kenzō Tange, "Architectural Research Team: Architectural Creation," *Shinkenchiku*, June 1956: 69–80.

Fig. 44
Kenzō Tange,
Hiroshima
Children's
Library

Fig. 45
Kenzō Tange,
Kagawa
Prefectural
Government
Office

POSTWAR ARCHITECTURE

Fig. 46
Kenzō Tange,
Kagawa
Prefectural
Office

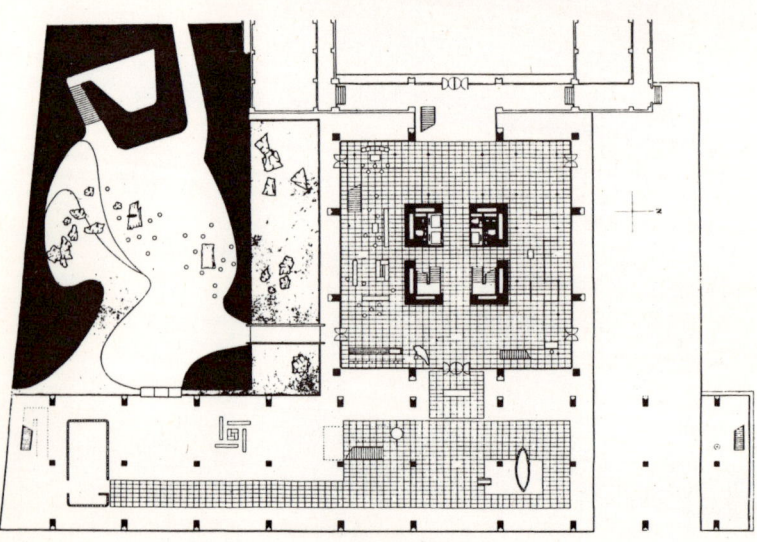

Fig. 47
Kenzō Tange,
Kagawa
Prefectural
Office

The complex (fig. 47) is made up of two geometrically simple volumes of contrasting forms and dimensions: a square and tall office building, and a low rectangular block for the assembly hall. The stereometry is disrupted by loggias which create, especially in the tall building, a continuous vibration of light that is counterpointed by concrete elements alluding to traditional wooden structures.

The powerful definition of the volumes is therefore offset by an expressiveness that seems to evoke the fragility of structures in ancient Japanese architecture. The juxtaposition of the two different historical dimensions acquires a particular importance by virtue of the fact that is clearly highlighted, not as a superimposition onto the building, but as an integral part of it. In the counterpoint created by the diverse volumes and the continuous vibration of the concrete members there is, however, an unresolved contrast. In effect, the reproduction in concrete of the memory of the timber structure has a certain mechanical quality that undermines the power of the architectural image. It is a contradiction that Tange himself would later find a way to overcome in works such as the Kurashiki City Hall.

"The Japanese architectural tradition is based on techniques and materials antithetical to reinforced concrete," Bruno Zevi writes. And he goes on:

> The material of the skeleton frame can easily be translated from wood into steel and in the transition, the artistic configuration of the lines and transparent panels do not undergo any radical alterations. But the expressive potential intrinsic to reinforced concrete is plastic, curved, and fluid. Using reinforced concrete in posts and beams as if it were steel means giving up trying to exploit the original potential of this "cast" material.[44]

But Zevi's view is too narrow. It fails to take into account the significance of the translation of timber elements into concrete in the buildings of the Peace Memorial Park or the Kagawa

Prefectural Office. At a distance of a few years, the evident ingenuity of those works appears as nothing more than a stage in a journey to maturity that has been completed at astonishing speed. The Kagawa building has a certain rigidity, in line with its didactic conception, but it nonetheless holds considerable interest as a steppingstone toward the more recent works of Tange and of Japanese modern architecture.

In the projects we have looked at so far, the structural element has been subordinate to the overall form; in other works, however, the structure itself becomes the main protagonist, the crucial element in a discourse that begins by glorifying the static functions and then goes on to reach higher and more complex degrees of expressiveness.

Particularly eloquent in this regard is the Shizuoka Convention Hall (1957) (figs. 48 and 49), in which the integration of structure and form gives the building an intensely dramatic quality: here, the residue of the technical details is absorbed and subsumed in the unity of the design.

Similarly, the broad vaulted ceiling of the Ehime Convention Hall at Matsuyama (fig. 50) gives its interior a very expressive feel, even if the exterior is far less assertive than usual, because of an overemphasis on the control of the structural elements.

In the Sogetsu Art Center in Tokyo (fig. 51) Tange adopts a quieter language that is in some ways reminiscent Le Corbusier's museum at Ahmedabad: in the block-like volume, clearly delineated by two robust horizontal bands of concrete, the main facade is punctured by apertures that highlight the massing, while the ribbon windows on the rear elevation are counterpointed by the powerful play of shadows generated by the prominent first-floor loggia. In this work, too, the tight integration of space, structure,

44  Bruno Zevi, "Un giapponese contro la tradizione," *L'Espresso*, September 20, 1959: 16. Moreover, as Boyd has remarked, the trabeated or beam-glorifying phase (the third) was a short-lived part of Tange's creative development. Boyd identifies the first phase in works that highlight simple forms alluding to traditional architecture, while the second is characterized by the expressive impetus based on advanced plastic forms and volumes, the third in the use of trabeated structures, and the fourth further develops the previous phase. See Robin Boyd, *Kenzō Tange* (New York: George Braziller, 1962), 32–33.

Fig. 48
Kenzō Tange,
Shizuoka
Convention
Hall

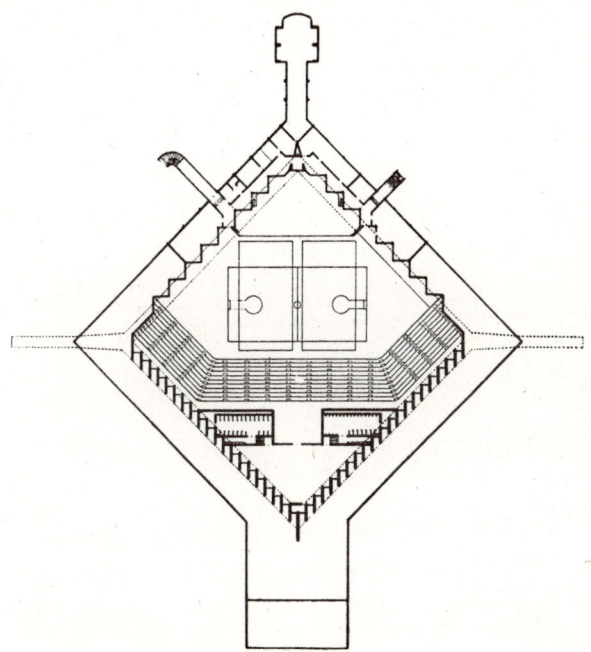

Fig. 49
Kenzō Tange,
Shizuoka
Convention Hall

POSTWAR ARCHITECTURE 109

Fig. 50
Kenzō Tange,
Ehime
Convention
Hall

Fig. 51
Kenzō Tange,
Sōgetsu Art
Center

Fig. 52
Kenzō Tange,
Sumi Memorial
Hall, Bisai

and details is a positive feature: here, the structural framework, based on a system of four massive pillars and double beams, is powerfully revealed on the exterior, foreshadowing the remarkable achievement of Kurashiki City Hall.

Another of Tange's more minor works is the Sumi complex at Bisai (fig. 52), designed to house the company's administrative offices and a public memorial hall. Here the usual rhythms of the office block are set against the strikingly bare surfaces and evident historicist allusions of the hall.

In the offices for the Dentsu advertising company in Osaka (fig. 53), Tange appears to be more rigorous in his spare treatment of the concrete grid of brise-soleils that defines the texture of the facade, where a series of incidental motifs—the two windowless floors for the radio and television studios, the gash of the entrance hall, and the superstructures containing the plant rooms—disrupt the monumental feel of the block, which is dominated, moreover, by symmetry and a strong contrast of light and shade. This is monumentality in the modern sense, again influenced by Le Corbusier, but in the Dentsu Building

Fig. 53
Kenzō Tange,
Dentsu Offices,
Osaka

it is not completely resolved due to an element of indecision or reticence in conceiving of the building as a single unitary mass—the very quality that would become the defining feature of his best works of recent years.

As Robin Boyd has pointed out,[45] the Imabari City Hall complex on the island of Shikoku marked a new phase in Tange's output. Designed in 1957 and completed in 1959, the complex —an office block and a public auditorium—draws on the same syntax as earlier works, but uses it in a way that is much more cogent and at the same time free, giving rise to a bolder language that can be seen as a prelude to the amazing expressive synthesis of the Kurashiki City Hall. Of particular interest is the spatial autonomy of the external facades of the auditorium: the superimposition of forms in recessed areas delimited by concrete fins suggests a line of experimentation that is by now largely unrelated to Corbusian models.

Tange's Kurashiki City Hall (figs. 54–57), completed in 1960,[46] was the first component of a larger redevelopment of the city's administrative center, part of a masterplan by architects Hideto Kishida and Eika Takayama that envisioned the restructuring of a large zone on the periphery and the conservation of the existing historic urban fabric.

The insertion of the new building into the historic fabric of the city is violent, brutal: the whole of the administrative center is treated as an organic unity, as if to underline the absolute incompatibility of modern democratic life with the ancient political and social structures embodied by the tradition-bound fabric all around it, a densely woven tissue of small single-family houses (fig. 54).

The first violent contrast evoked by Tange is thus one of scale. The cityscape created by the completed complex—the two large unitary volumes of the City Hall and the auditorium

---

45    Boyd, *Kenzō Tange*, 34.
46    Situated at the edge of the historical center of the city, the completed complex was made up of the City Hall, a vast square, and an auditorium that was built immediately after the City Hall and also designed by Tange.

Fig. 54
Kenzō Tange, Kurashiki City Hall

encamped in a large open space that is not related in any way to the surrounding city—is charged with a dramatic tension. It makes an urgent appeal to all the people of Kurashiki to consider critically their own condition as citizens of Japan and to choose between a modern way of life and traditional structures.

The violence of the architectural expression can therefore be seen as the restatement, in form, of a polemical intention, enacted with a coherence that is hard to find in European or American architecture, the case of Le Corbusier excepted. In the Kurashiki project, figural intensity and ideological engagement come together to such a degree that the architecture could be defined as "epic," aimed at "forcing decisions rather than eliciting sentiments." Having chosen the way of violence, Tange takes it to extremes. Given his all-consuming interest in demonstrating his thesis, a reduction to the essential becomes

Fig. 55
Kenzō Tange,
Kurashiki City
Hall

indispensable. The buildings are modelled as two large volumes, distinguished by their individual geometries (a parallelepiped for the City Hall and a truncated parallelepiped for the auditorium) and set in a relation that is mediated by the large square, which both unites them and gives them the appearance of two large *objets trouvés*.⁴⁷

Essentiality is also the principle informing the organization of the City Hall. Raised on substantial pillars at a few concentrated points, and ordered by a uniform 1.8m module,

---

47  In a lecture at the University of Hawaii, Tange gave his view of what the public wants: "People want castles where they live in. They want castles where they work in. They want eternal and more durable feeling. They do not want weakness or tentativeness, but this weak and tentative feeling that we have in our tradition sometimes appears in the so-called modern architecture of the world," quoted in Boyd, *Kenzō Tange*, 38. We cannot, therefore, agree with Boyd, who sees the "citizens' hall" as "the most disturbing element of the building." Philip Thiel offers a much more interesting perspective: "The nexus of the ideas which animate postwar Japanese architecture is most clearly seen in the public buildings that have come into being in the course of the reconstruction of the war-damaged cities. The resolution of this new force of democracy with the old force of tradition is expressed in these buildings, and particularly in the many new city halls and prefectural office buildings which are the chief symbols of the new corporate life. Kenzō Tange's new city hall for old Kurashiki can thus be examined as vector of change in a culture now challenged with the need for new common symbols. As an expressive work of art consciously made impressive to underline the importance of the democratic processes and public services therein housed, it and the evolving plans for its urban context merit attention." Philip Thiel, "City Hall at Kurashiki, Japan," *Architectural Review*, no. 780 (February 1962).

Fig. 56
Kenzō Tange,
Kurashiki City
Hall, lobby

the simple structure defines a block that is entirely unitary, precise, and synthetic in its volumetric arrangement and functional layout. At the same time, the building echoes classical motifs, both through the absolute symmetry that radiates from the double-height central hall into the assembly hall above, and through the sharp geometric form of the outdoor auditorium that soars up from the roof.

But then this volumetric compactness is disrupted, in an apparent attempt at stripped down decoration, by the treatment of the surfaces and the design of the facades, where the window slits inserted seemingly randomly into the continuous concrete planks create a dense play of light and shadow (fig. 55). The slits—appearing as flaws in the regular horizontal mesh of the concrete—effectively underscore the formal unity of the exterior walls. It is a unity defined by the patterns made by light as it moves over a surface in which solids and voids are integrated, giving rise to a complex interplay of forms that enhances the powerful massing.

The dialectic between this refined surface texture and the massive horizontal beam at the base of the building (echoed at the top by the load-bearing beam that forms the parapet of the upper terrace) creates a dramatic tension that is only resolved by the exceptionally unitary nature of the building.

Kurashiki City Hall is one of Tange's finest buildings and one of the greatest works of Japanese architecture in recent years, a significant stage in the attempt to develop an expressive "eloquence" through the in-depth study of a rigorous figurative theme. Here, too, a resolute, violent, brutal idea of a new city order is combined with memory, with an appeal—an invitation, almost—to reinterpret the values of tradition within the framework of a new vision of the world, a new social order. In this context, the elegant, complex interplay of the facades, with the concrete planking echoing the texture of wood, does not appear rhetorical or out of tune with the powerful massing of the volume or the overall urban composition. Tange writes:

Fig. 57
Kenzō Tange,
Kurashiki
City Hall,
boardroom

Japanese tradition cannot continue to live on its own strengths, nor can it be considered as the sole source of creative energy. For the spirit of its evolution to become dynamic, I believe that we must first reject and destroy tradition. We are seeking a new freedom of expression, one able to stand as a symbol of a society emancipated from theocratic regimes ... Rather than a logical structure, we are looking for an equilibrium of plastic form.[48]

48 Tange often criticized pure functionalism. But when arguing against it, he overstated the case for the values of the image, considered to be the typical means for innovative action, which he believed to be the principal duty of architecture.

Fig. 58
Kenzō Tange,
World Health
Organization
Headquarters,
Geneva,
competition
entry

The recovery of history through a decisive break with the past—one of Tange's main aims—is fully accomplished in the Kurashiki City Hall, which bears no trace of the allegorical references that were still latent in the Kagawa Prefecture and the Dentsu Building.

An equally aggressive plasticity defines Tange's entry to the international design competition for the new World Health Organization Headquarters in Geneva (fig. 58). Though he did not win the competition—the emphatic figuration of the project was unlikely to find favor with a jury that had strong rationalist leanings—he was undoubtedly the moral victor.[49] The project for Geneva, too, is suffused with a potent symbolic charge. Once again, the structure plays a crucial figurative role: two powerful curved concrete blocks form the frame of the structure, creating a triangular cross-section of rare energy.

By comparison, one of Tange's more recent works, the Totsuka Country Club House in Tokyo, appears less coherent (fig. 59). The project is nonetheless interesting as it provides a ready means of analyzing the limits and the risks of the complex position of the new school of architects.

49    The invited competition was won by the Swiss architect Jean Tschumi. See *L'architettura cronache e storia*, no. 62 (1960): 546–49.

What the Country Club House clearly shows is that "brutalist" mannerism has become worn out, and not on account of an inherent weakness in its poetics or underlying methodology, but rather because of a dilution of the expressive intensity with which the experiment is pursued. This may at first seem to be a formalist criticism, but a closer look shows its relevance to the project in question. In fact, the expressive vehemence of Tange's architecture, and its structural exertions, are only valid when they are rooted in a pressing social issue and make a high-level contribution to the ongoing discourse. In the Country Club House, Tange is experimenting with the application of his poetics to a socially anodyne theme, looking at what changes need to be made to the syntax in this transition from works that are exceptional—in terms of their role in the urban fabric or their intrinsic functional features—to the commonplace themes of current architecture.

The Totsuka Country Club House makes apparent the difficulties involved in that transition. While maintaining the usual organization of the elements of his architectural elements, Tange tries to apply them to a plainer structural configuration, as if to demonstrate that the methodology could be extended without the loss of its essential expressive qualities. The result is a formalism completely stripped of polemical force, which is now only alluded to, weakly, in some of the individual elements. The exaggeration of the load-bearing structure—the six massive, plastically modeled pillars and the broad curving roof that dominates the building—seems strangely unrelated to its overall organization or to the definition of its other formal elements.

It is the loss of the symbolic power of these images that makes Tange's experiment a failure—one that is not to be attributed to the architect's supposed integration into a system, but that rather reveals the dangers of a slackening of expressive energy. To sum up this implicit criticism of Tange's methodology: it is hardly possible to extend, as universally applicable, a working method that relies on emotional intensity. And this also constitutes the limits of a Japanese new school that draws

Fig. 59
Kenzō Tange,
Totsuka Country
Club House

Fig. 60
Kenzō Tange,
Atami Hotel,
Tokyo

its raison d'être, as we have already noted, from mannerism—a mannerism that becomes more viable when it operates at a common level, but that still leaves room, at the risk of a possible *saturation of images*, for some exceptional elements.

A similar criticism could be levelled at the Atami Hotel in Tokyo, completed in 1962, a casual, superficial work that betrays a cool tempering of Tange's poetics (fig. 60).

In his urban planning projects, however, Tange manages to stretch, if not go beyond, the limits of his own methodology, as we will see below. Indeed, it could be argued that his most recent urban-scale works show him continually renewing his own approach to design. Among them, there is the new building for Dentsu, which incorporates a small-scale version of the fishbone-like structure elaborated in the plan for Tokyo, or the covered stadium for the 1964 Olympics, which follows the Rikkyō University Library (1961), where Tange tackled the problem of highlighting some of the figurative aspects of the historic campus setting into which the building was to be inserted.

In Tange's most recent work, the Nichinan Cultural Center (fig. 1), we see a plasticity that is more aggressive than in any of his other buildings. Here, the mass of exposed reinforced concrete is torn apart and its surfaces pierced with random, overwrought apertures that contrast with crudely protruding rainspouts: all contribute to a play of volumes that is rather like a work of *art informel* (the critic Yūichirō Kōjirō likened the effect of these surfaces to a chance process of erosion). The effect is reprised in the interior of the auditorium, where the stage curtain, decorated by Tōkō Shinoda's action painting, accords perfectly with Tange's accentuated spatiality.

## 7. Kunio Maekawa and the MID group

There are obvious affinities between the output of the Tange Lab and the experiments undertaken from 1955 on by Maekawa and his team of young architects, who go by the name of MID or MIDO [English spelling and Japanese pronunciation, respectively].[50] This group continues to develop professionally: besides Masato Ōtaka, who has already been mentioned, it includes the highly skilled Azusa Kito. But rather than dwelling on the common features of the two groups, it is more interesting to look at their different roles in Japanese architectural discourse.

Where Tange's work may be considered as a catalyst, a driving force, Maekawa's personal talent and past career mark him out as a pole of distillation, a critical thinker, and hands-on practitioner. Though no less vehement in its expression, Maekawa's architecture appears more balanced over the course of his career, more consistent in terms of the intrinsic features of the individual buildings, even as they were modulated with his shift from rationalism to the brutalist language of the new school. Nonetheless, the MID group that has gathered around him shares another element in common with Tange's team: the need to forge a close link between the innovative figural expression of the building and the general progress of Japanese society. The young architects of Ōtaka's and Kito's generation have received a democratic education. They share the ideals of the popular movements that are attempting to bring about radical social transformation, and with their buildings they seek to express, even anticipate, this social change.

In a recent interview published in an Indian journal,[51] Maekawa claimed:

> Modern architecture is architecture for humanity and I believe that we must never forget that the much more

---

50   Masato Ōtaka, Ichirō Kawahara, Toshiya Tajima, Keiichi Okumura, Saburo Ōsawa, Kosaburo Sakitani, Ryōhei Amamiya, and Joji Yokoyama.
51   Quoted in *Architecture d'aujourd'hui*, no. 98 (1961): 20.

serious and difficult task is the humanization of modern civilizations whose principal features, such as mass production, mass communications, leisure time, and culture dominate humanity like uncontainable giants.

Architecture is thus seen as a means of guiding and developing society, as an embodiment of the demands of these cultural movements in the face of a civilization that seems to have completely lost its way. The young Japanese critic Noburo Kawazoe writes:

> While a functionalist gives the concept of time and space to nature and forcefully adapts modern form to Japanese reality, Ōtaka and his group [MID] are in search of an architecture which grows out of reality, like a tree with its roots deep in fertile ground. Rather than a recognition of Japanese technical inferiority, this involves the creation of a higher technique by using existing methods. It involves a refusal to copy tradition as well as a refusal to use imported techniques and materials without fully digesting them ... Again, since architecture is not the result of labor producing exchange value but the result of work producing utility value, it is essential to nullify the deleterious effects of the capitalist system on Asiatic production and to organize architecture into modern work. This is the problem facing the Japanese architectural world.[52]

The Fukushima Cultural Center (fig. 61), completed in 1958 for the Japanese Teachers Union (one of the most progressive in the country), had a tight budget and an emphasis on function, given the complex requirements of the multipurpose hall.

52   Noboru Kawazoe, "Modern Japanese Architecture Confronts Functionalism: New Buildings of Japan," *Zodiac*, no. 3 (1958): 140–46. Translation emended. In the same article, Kawazoe gives his own interpretation of the importance of tradition in modern Japanese architecture: "In postwar Japan, where natural resources are scarce and the internal market small, the majority of big industries subsist on technical co-operation and the introduction of foreign capital. Thus, economic circles are colonial in their nature. Consequently, the entire industry is superficial in its nature. It is in opposition to the colonization of modern civilization that traditionalism gained power."

Fig. 61
Kunio Maekawa,
Fukushima
Education
Center

The building exploits the full structural and figural potential of the concrete technology, even if the vigorous plasticity of its undulating roof and the corrugated load-bearing surfaces has a certain unwarranted baroque quality—a quality accentuated, moreover, by the mechanical juxtaposition of the low block containing the offices and smaller spaces with the agitated mass of the auditorium. Despite these reservations, it cannot be denied that the building opens up wider expressive horizons: the critic Kazuo Hayama acknowledged as much soon after its completion, when he underlined its synthesis of social content and figural expression, describing it as a *new realism*.

If the Fukushima Cultural Center represented a break that was not yet perfectly controlled, in the Harumi Apartments in Tokyo, completed the following year, Maekawa and his team realized a work that was fully mature in every regard, a rare example of collective-type housing in Japan (fig. 62). Maekawa had been appointed by a semi-public housing association to design experimental multi-story housing as part of a major residential development serving a port-industrial area. However, only one block was built, either because of a failure to grasp the progressive

Fig. 62
Kunio Maekawa,
Harumi
Apartments,
Tokyo

Fig. 63
Kunio Maekawa,
Harumi
Apartments,
Tokyo

aspects of Maekawa's design or because of a deliberate campaign against him. Instead, the district would gradually be filled with nondescript five-story buildings of poor architectural quality. Once more, then, an ambitious methodological model was rejected and made to seem like a defiant "monument."

The expressionistic brutality of this work, together with its absolute figurative coherence, make it one of the most important and emblematic examples of modern Japanese architecture. The block proposes a new way of life, a new urban dimension, and constitutes a precise, vehement critique of a form of housing that is not so much traditional as thoroughly anachronistic—but in doing so, it recovers the qualities of that tradition which remain sound. In their presentation of the project, Ichirō Kawahara and Masato Ōtaka write:

> The density and confusion of the city of Tokyo give little hope for a new way of living together in a community. We can find some privacy in the residential sector of the hilly section of Tokyo and a spirit of cooperation in downtown apartments, where people live frugally with an open heart. Our purpose was therefore to build an apartment where privacy and the spirit of cooperation coexist.[53]

The robust, summary lines of the concrete slab of the Harumi building emphasize both its size and its structural quality, while the housing cells draw inspiration from, but at the same time strikingly redefine, the typical spaces of the traditional Japanese house (fig. 63).

The different ways of treating the overall form of the building and the living spaces correspond to the different functions for which they are designed. On the urban scale, the building forms a powerful new configuration that establishes a direct relationship with the city, with the surrounding environment, while the individual apartments, through their scale and function, seek

---

53  Ichirō Kawahara and Masato Ōtaka, "Toward a New Living Space," *Shinkenchiku*, no. 1 (1957): 23.

more to revive or at least reinterpret ways of living that can be preserved if they are set into the right context.[54]

The new Kyoto Civic Center confirms a predilection of the part of Maekawa for schemes that are related to or gathered around defined open spaces (fig. 64).[55] The building is inserted into an urban fabric of low-rise housing, and forms, together with a nearby museum and a municipal library, a major cultural hub. As usual, the relationship with the city is the main factor determining Maekawa's aesthetic choices as well as the functional program. On this occasion, the architect opts for a form that is extremely compact, and largely undifferentiated, a little higher than the existing buildings around it, but much more extensive. Distilled into a single continuous volume, the three components that make up the complex—concert hall (2,500 seats), theater (1,300 seats), and conference hall—are arranged around a vast open courtyard.

The simple, uniform massing is accentuated by the continuous, strongly projecting eaves line, which weights down the entire complex, so it appears to hug the ground, and minimizes the height differences between the blocks. The massing is then complicated, however, by the terraces that project at different levels, creating pauses and dynamic breaks in the cleanly delineated profile of the building. Rather than falling into step with, or mimicking, the "ambience" of the existing environment, the design of the roof, balustrade, expansion joints, and glazing all hint at an ineffable style rooted in the history of modern Japan, but now couched in a decidedly new language.

---

54   Kawahara and Ōtaka, "Toward a New Living Space," 24. Kawahara and Ōtaka go on to say: "As Japanese architects we must admit that the private Japanese apartment based on the tatami is in contradiction with modern life. With all the social problems involved, tradition and contemporary life are in opposition day after day. The differences are usually resolved with a compromise: most postwar residential buildings are the result of this compromise. Investigating the value of tradition, moreover, we have done our best to resolve this contrast. We have thus aimed at a completely new way of life, outside all compromises, and we have concentrated all our efforts on reaching that objective."

55   We have translated the Japanese term *kaikan* with "civic center"; it literally means a "meeting place" and is usually a multipurpose facility (similar to English festival halls) with various auditoriums and rooms for conferences, meetings, concerts, etc.

Fig. 64
Kunio Maekawa,
Kyoto Civic
Center

In contrast to the uniform exterior, the internal spaces are highly differentiated: especially the large foyer (fig. 65), where a symmetrical layout and restrained but clever interplay of stairs creates a highly expressive modern representative space.

In 1960 Maekawa and his group completed the construction of the new campus for Gakushuin University in Tokyo, a private institution, one of the oldest in Japan, with an aristocratic tradition (figs. 66 and 67).⁵⁶ This major work explores the same expressive theme tackled in the Kyoto Civic Center and later the Tokyo Metropolitan Festival Hall in Ueno Park. Here, too, there was no possibility of a dialogue with the surrounding urban fabric or structures, given the unbridgeable gulf between the cultural and social premises of the new intervention and those of the historic buildings (a gulf further widened, in this instance, by the difference between the old, classicist tradition of teaching and the new demands of democratic pedagogy).

In response, the new campus buildings are largely self-contained, both in form and plan, giving rise to a tight composition with a strong, unitary character that nonetheless

Fig. 65
Kunio Maekawa,
Kyoto Civic
Center

accommodates the potential for future change, even suggesting a possible basis for complete redevelopment. Two parallel blocks—the new institutes for science and the humanities—define the outer edges of the intervention. Each is connected to a square administrative block, which is in turn linked to the large pyramid containing the auditorium. Condensing, gathering the other buildings around it, the mass of the auditorium gives an identity to the whole complex. Its stark geometric form—which is barely glossed by the design of the concrete cladding, the few apertures, and the plinth structure—appears as a kind of expressive hinge in dialectical counterpoint to the simple but finely wrought facades of the institutes, with their recessed elements (fig. 68).

Again, the influence of Le Corbusier is evident in the aesthetic choices, and especially in the modulation of the facades and the relations between the various buildings. But in the interior of the auditorium, with its expansive and controlled

56   Gakushuin University is one of fifty universities in Tokyo.

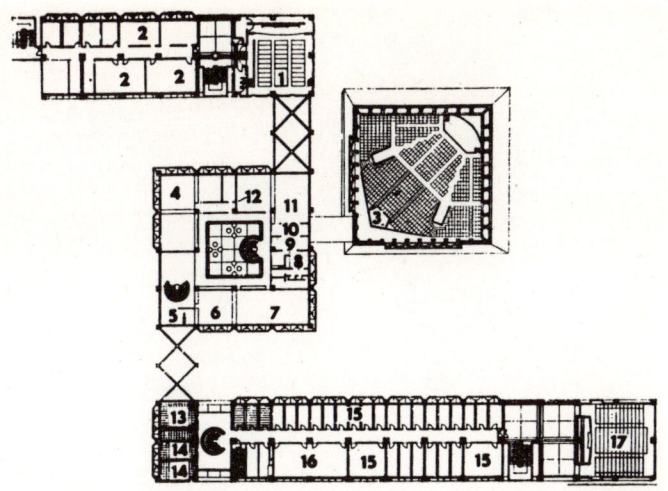

Fig. 66
Kunio Maekawa,
Gakushuin
University,
Tokyo, plan
a) first floor
b) second floor

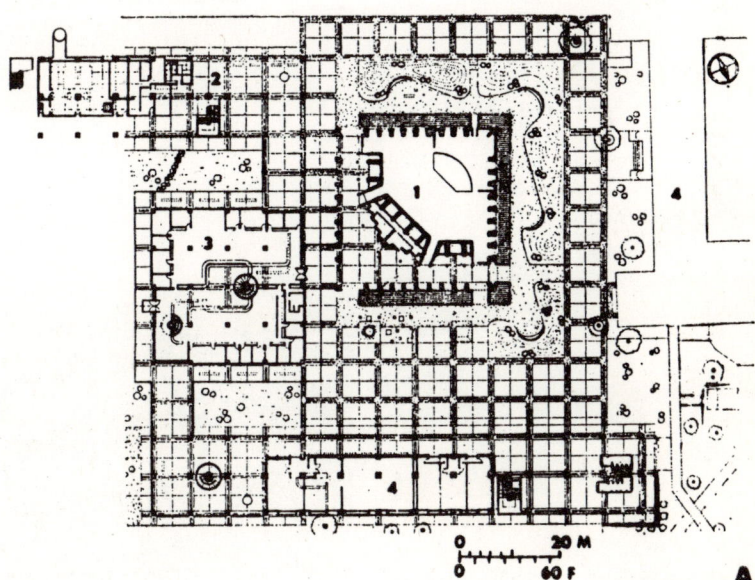

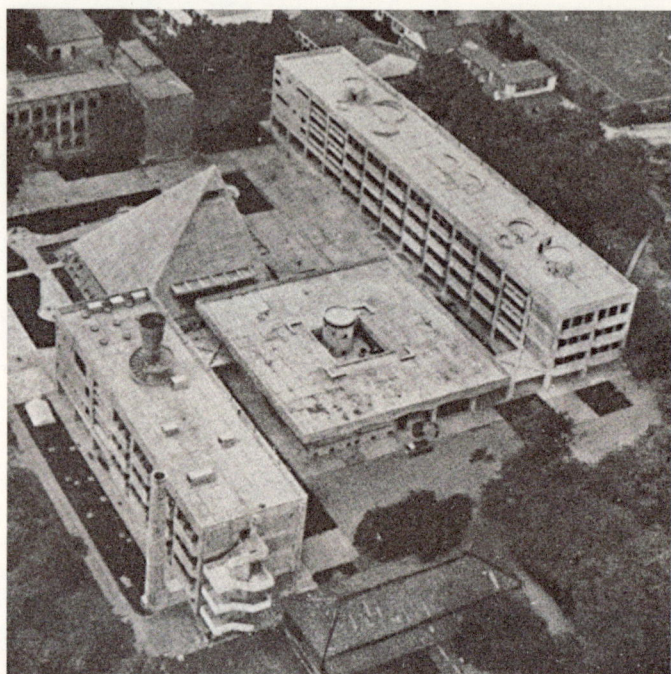

Fig. 67
Kunio Maekawa,
Gakushuin
University,
Tokyo

Fig. 68
Kunio Maekawa,
Gakushuin
University,
Tokyo, facade
detail of the
Institute of
Humanities

spatiality, its carefully studied lighting, and its structure played out in a decorative key, we see a highly original interpretation of the French master's teachings that confirms the value of having an ideal model, a point of reference that can be reflected on, critiqued, time and time again. Through this, each form, each modulation, each detail enters into a unifying discourse in which the relation between the exterior space and the spatiality of the individual elements is defined by a single expressive intent.

Maekawa's masterpiece, however, is undoubtedly the Tokyo Metropolitan Festival Hall in Ueno Park, one of the most expressive pieces of architecture in Japan today. Before we consider it, however, we need to first look at another building in that park.

The Japanese government asked Le Corbusier to design a museum to house the Matsukata Collection of western art when it returned to Japan from Paris, where it had been sequestered during the war. The chosen site was Ueno Park, which was already home to the museums of natural history, fine arts, and science.

Within this park, on a site that had sweeping views over the city of Tokyo, Le Corbusier envisioned a complex that contained not only the National Museum of Western Art but also a pavilion for temporary exhibitions and a theater for experimental performances, which he called a *boîte à miracles*. Following his usual method of composition, he conceived a dialogue between the buildings as objects—as geometrically distinct forms that define an essentially closed figural space—as can be seen in the preliminary sketches published in the *Oeuvre complète* (fig. 69).[57] However, the original idea was diluted as only the museum was built—realized by three of his former students, Maekawa, Sakakura, and Yoshizaka (fig. 70). In this sense, the juxtaposition of Le Corbusier's work and Maekawa's Festival Hall (one of the best examples of Japanese architecture, as we have said) is not particularly felicitous.

For the museum in Tokyo Le Corbusier reprised his famous study of 1939, offering an updated version of his *musée à spirale*

57  Le Corbusier, *Oeuvre complète, 1952–1957* (Zurich: Editions d'Architecture, 1957), 168–73.

Fig. 69
Le Corbusier, sketch for the National Museum of Western Art, Tokyo

Fig. 70
Le Corbusier, National Museum of Western Art, Tokyo

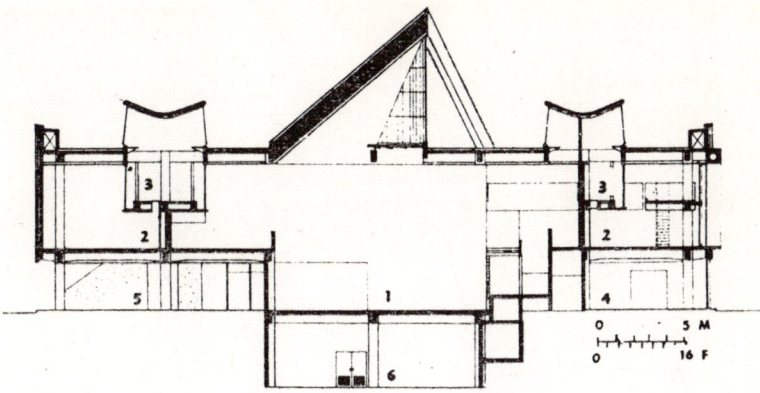

Fig. 71
Le Corbusier,
National
Museum of
Western Art,
Tokyo, section

*carrée* (square spiral museum), now stripped of its potential for unlimited extension. The space is a closed parallelepiped, uniform and elementary on the outside, evocatively fragmented and hollowed out on the inside, with the kind of expressive modulations that had already been tried out to greater effect in the museum at Ahmedabad (fig. 71).

Like the museum in India, the one in Tokyo has a central full-height space for the sculptures and, gathered around it, a series of ramps that lead to the picture galleries (fig. 72). All the attention is thus focused on the interior, where the play of volumes and light cascading from large skylights has the potential to form a unitary whole together with the works on display —a potential that is not properly exploited by the current arrangement.

The area in front of Le Corbusier's museum is now occupied by Maekawa's recently completed Festival Hall, which brings together a vast auditorium for concerts, opera, ballet, etc., a smaller hall for international conferences and experimental performances, a music library, an exhibition space, and a restaurant (fig. 73). The guiding principle of the design appears to have been to achieve a rigorous overall unity through a heightened differentiation of the individual parts. The building's character as a great machine, then, is perfectly consistent with its role as

Fig. 72
Le Corbusier, National Museum of Western Art, Tokyo, interior

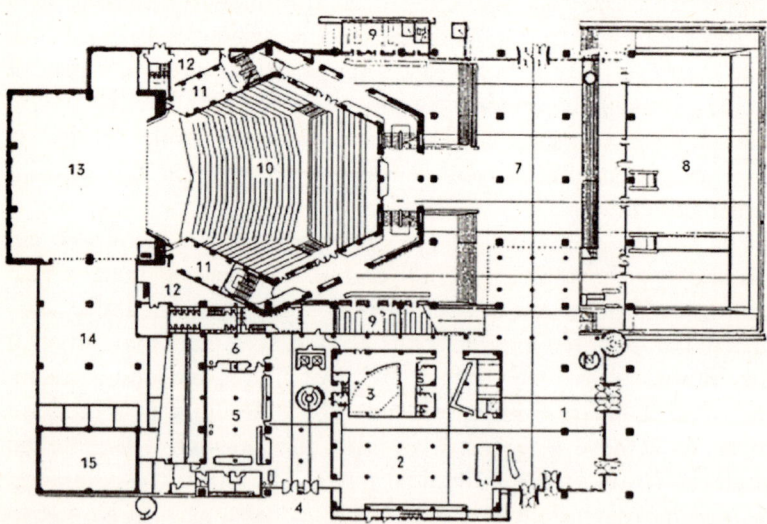

Fig. 73
Kunio Maekawa, Tokyo Metropolitan Festival Hall, plan of auditorium level

a multipurpose cultural center. The syncretism of the centralized plan—expressed in the way the tops of the various halls emerge through the roof slab, like objects set on a gigantic tray—is matched by the geometric fragmentation of the counterposed elements. It is as if the architecture had weathered a cataclysm that had ripped apart its compact unity but left behind enough evidence for its original form to still be recognized (figs. 74 and 75).

The expressive quality of the building is thus defined by the deliberate contrast (heightened by every means) between the various *fragments* that make up the complex. Unlike the Kyoto Civic Center, where each hall, each space, each function is characterized by its own highly individual geometric order, the volumes here are reduced to the essential, but are overlapped and juxtaposed to create a vigorous expressive tension.

The unifying role is then played by the vast roof slab from which the geometric forms of the halls emerge, albeit in a way tends to accentuate rather than subdue the drama. Seen from below, the large roof slab appears as a striking convex form. Together with the base of the building—which is punctured in places by a dense series of concrete sun-shading elements that contrast with the roof's powerful plasticity—it generates a potent tension that is calmed in the upper part of the building, with its expansive unitary surfaces and freely articulated volumes.

Maekawa seems to want to create in the viewer a kind of psychological tension, forcing them to continually move their gaze from the powerful figural synthesis to the fragmented detail, from the emphatic geometry and brutalist construction of the constituent elements of the center (one could note here the dramatic contrast between the concrete roof slab and the marble volume of the large auditorium) to the elaborate interplay of individual details, each conceived with particular care, but all designed to be absorbed into the overall unity of the complex.

The continuity runs through the interior and exterior. The powerful spatial configuration of the grand foyer is enhanced by the treatment of the floor with its subtle, discontinuous

Fig. 74
Kunio Maekawa,
Tokyo Metropolitan Festival Hall

Fig. 75
Kunio Maekawa,
Tokyo Metropolitan Festival Hall

Fig. 76
Kunio Maekawa, Tokyo Metropolitan Festival Hall, main hall

patterns, by the texture of the walls, and by the play of light from the spotlights and square fixtures that are artfully scattered across the flat ceiling.

Conversely, the interior of the large hexagonal auditorium is characterized by the contrast between the geometric clarity of the interior space and the fragmented quality of the walls covered with Ryokichi Mukai's sculptures, which also play an acoustic role (fig. 76). The sculptor's stated intention was to bring in a sense of movement to counter the massive, unitary feel of the auditorium:

> Ultimately, I chose an organic design that was diametrically opposed to the straight lines and geometric curves of the building. At the same time, I wanted to avoid anything bizarre that might seem remote from human life and feelings, or give people that strange feeling of not belonging—the kind of feeling that arises when you are suddenly confronted with your own reflection in a show window on the streets of a foreign city. As I understand it,

Fig. 77
Kunio Maekawa, Tokyo Metropolitan Festival Hall, recital hall

the concept that underlies this building is that of a great psychological symphony embracing all the incongruities of human life. I felt that if my murals could retain their original form in this vastness, then I would have fulfilled my responsibility.[58]

However, the contrast appears overexaggerated and, combined with the intrinsic quality of the sculptures, which are clearly inspired by Arp, it means the work does not mesh with the overall expression of the architecture, in contrast to the success of the smaller hall, where Masayuki Nagare starts from the idea of working with the concrete surfaces of the wall, folding and molding his material to create a merging of abstract figures and architectural form that is perfectly in keeping with the spirit of Maekawa's work (fig. 77).

58    Ryokichi Mukai, "On the Sculptural Acoustic Walls in the Main Auditorium," *Japan Architect*, June–July 1961: 34. Translation modified.

Inevitably, the completion of such an important, culturally resonant building sparked bitter controversy, renewing the tension in the long-running debate that began with Tange's early projects. Representing one faction, Antonin Raymond argued that Maekawa's work is a perfect fusion of function and expression that signals a new way forward for contemporary architecture.[59] In the other camp, Kiyoshi Higuchi fiercely criticized the complex as a wanton break with the past, seeing it as nothing more than a collection of fine surfaces and decoration and a symptom of the—regrettable, in his view—spread of the Corbusian manner.[60]

However, even the critics cannot discount the remarkable expressive power of the Tokyo Metropolitan Festival Hall, which has been a great success with the general public, being named the most popular new building of 1961 in a survey published by *Japan Architect*.

Maekawa has not achieved the same expressive coherence in his more recent works, either in the competition to design the cathedral for the Roman Catholic Archdiocese of Tokyo (won by Tange with a project that is among his least convincing), or in the Yokohama Youth Center, in which he seems to lapse into a pale mannerist imitation of himself.

59  Antonin Raymond, "Tokyo Metropolitan Festival Hall," *Japan Architect*, June–July 1961: 49.
60  Kiyoshi Higuchi, "A Second Plea: Architecture is More Than Aesthetic Form," *Japan Architect*, June–July 1961: 50. What probably irritates those who criticize the formalism in Maekawa's work is the uninhibited way he intuitively relates form and function. Like Tange, Maekawa uncouples the aesthetic discourse from a strict dependence on function and achieves the synthesis by giving his architecture qualities that go beyond the contingent limits of the various set themes.

## 8. Junzō Sakakura

If Tange is the boldest innovator in Japanese architectural culture, and Maekawa the one who has advanced the development and critical exploration of its new language of forms, then Sakura, the third master of the new school, is more concerned than the others to define a style that can be widely applied, drawing on a simpler design methodology.

Undoubtedly a more modest personality than Tange or Maekawa, Sakakura is also more concerned with a harmony that could be termed classical in the best sense of the word. His works embody a remarkable continuity. Throughout his career —from the Paris Pavilion (1936) to the Kamakura Museum of Modern Art (1951) and his recently completed works—he has constantly sought a classical sense of unity within the scope of the techniques and ideals of the modern movement. His notable achievements speak of an approach that, far from being gratuitous or escapist, is imbued with a strength of conviction. The works may be charged with less expressive intensity, but they are no less effective or potent for it.

The completion of the Kamakura Museum was followed by a period of reduced activity, when Sakakura devoted himself mainly to interiors and the construction of single-family homes. Already in the Hashima Town Hall at Gifu (1959), however, we see an accomplished expression of his modern classicism—one that tellingly reveals both the virtues and the limits of his architectural vision (fig. 78). In the composition of the volumes of the building and its reflecting pool, Sakakura manages both to define the individual elements and incidental forms (for example, through the play of the curved roofs on top of the building) and to establish an overall unity. And the way he does this is not through an exaggeration of the structure, but through finding an equilibrium between the various elements. In this instance, the relationship with tradition is somewhat overstated, laid bare by the weak connection between the horizontal loggias and the schematically arranged, calm glazed surfaces.

Fig. 78
Junzō Sakakura,
Hajima Town
Hall

Fig. 79
Junzō Sakakura,
Silk Center,
Yokohama

POSTWAR ARCHITECTURE

Fig. 80
Junzō Sakakura,
Civic Cultural
Center, Ueno

The Silk Center at Yokohama, from the same year, is much less refined but still displays a powerful, concise plasticity (fig. 79). Here, the overall compositional approach seems inspired by Tange's civic buildings, and by the Kagawa Prefecture in particular. The concrete structure is exposed and highlighted in the four-story lower block, while the upper part of the building is modeled by continuous loggias which create a play of shadow and light that tempers the deliberate roughness of the structure and its schematic contrasts. The aesthetic effect, though rather contrived, is nonetheless masterfully handled.

A more representative example of Sakakura's architectural vision can be found in the Civic Cultural Center in Ueno (1963), so far the only element to be realized of a larger municipal complex that Sakakura has envisioned for this provincial town (fig. 80). In this work, he looks for a solution that is unitary in terms of both structure and function. A multipurpose hall, 20 x 20m, is covered by a hyperbolic-paraboloid concrete shell supported on four concrete pillars that are extrapolated from the square envelope of the hall. Out of this pile up of elements—structural frame, opaque walls, glazing—he creates a sober, balanced figural composition, a place for social exchange based on a sound conception of democracy. Indeed, as Sakura himself acknowledges, it is these smaller-scale projects that seem best suited to the expression of his quiet but engaged architectural poetics.

In his many single-family houses, Sakakura to some extent continues the approach he began with the International House

Fig. 81
Junzō Sakakura,
Shionogi
Research
Institute,
Osaka

in Tokyo (1955), but enriches it with new elements, as seen in the high standards of construction and the way he mediates a traditional lifestyle and a modern functionality, bringing them together in a highly refined, calm synthesis.

At Saijo Municipal Gymnasium (1961), Sakakura's solution to the problem of a large suspended prestressed concrete roof slab was to deploy a parabolic model that had been tested in the US and Europe (for example in the Black Forest Hall in Karlsruhe or the Congress Hall in Berlin) but had not yet been used in Japan. The resulting structure has a self-assured rigor, notwithstanding some unfortunate details.

Two other recent buildings—which are among the most interesting new constructions in Japan—reveal a further shift, with Sakakura's tempered expressiveness acquiring a tension unknown in his previous works.

In the first of these buildings, Kure City Hall (1961), the civic schema introduced by Tange is enriched and made more complex by its fragmentation: the curved volumes of the reception spaces are set in deliberate contrast to the purist geometry of the tall office block, to which they are linked by a low walkway on *pilotis*.

The design of the second building, the Shionogi Research Institute in Osaka (1962), is more rigorous and more effective (fig. 81). In these pharmaceutical laboratories, Sakakura again makes use of contrasts, but between surfaces this time, rather than volumes. While the walls that frame an inner trapezoidal courtyard space are fragmented (evidently in the manner of Le Corbusier), the end walls are solid and clad in blue-green majolica tiles—an accomplished synthesis of refinement and the non-finite that does not strive for drama and yet embodies something close to a modern monumentality.

Precisely because his style is less inflected by emotion, Sakakura solves the problem that we described as a possible symptom of regression in Tange's latest works. Sakakura, too, has designed unique works that break with the traditional context, and, importantly, his method has the potential for widespread application, albeit at the cost of a lower level of expressiveness.

## 9. Current architecture (1957–63)

"The advantage for the Japanese in today's transitional development," Walter Gropius wrote on his return from a stay in Japan,

> seems to be that they are still attuned to and in the presence of perfect examples of the balance achieved between individual initiative and voluntary subordination to a common principle. This should enable them to make the otherwise so painful and difficult transition from a handicraft to a machine culture with greater ease and without the loss of orientation, direction, and tradition which is threatening so many other societies.[61]

Gropius concluded:

> The Japanese architect, in particular, faces the almost insoluble task of having to house a population whose way of life, particularly in the cities, is in the process of a far-reaching transformation. Not only is he forced to work within very limited means, he is also frustrated by the fact that the compromise between traditional Japanese and the modern western living habits, which is unavoidable nowadays, presents him with the most difficult psychological and technical problems.[62]

In an attempt to resolve these psychological and technical problems, young Japanese architects are breaking with the past in an increasingly dramatic way. While looking, in almost all cases, to the teachings of the masters of the new school, they are producing a torrent of decidedly revolutionary proposals for new ways of living and organizing space. To understand the

---

61    Walter Gropius, "Architecture in Japan," in Walter Gropius, Kenzō Tange, and Yasuhiro Ishimoto, *Katsura: Tradition and Creation in Japanese Architecture* (New Haven: Yale University Press, 1960), 2.
62    Gropius, "Architecture in Japan," 10–11.

objectives pursued by the new generation, it may be useful to summarize the terms of a debate that ran from 1960 to 1961 and involved American critics on one side, and Japanese critics and architects on the other.

In August 1960, *House Beautiful* published a monographic issue dedicated to Japan, significantly titled *shibui*. Completely untranslatable, *shibui* is an adjective that expresses synthetically the spirit of the oriental cultural tradition: it indicates a way of being and a way of expressing oneself figuratively that is at once objective but not detached, profound but not tragic, calm but not inert, beautiful but not ostentatious, new but substantially bound to tradition, something unusual and original that has the patina created by a long development over time—a time that is in turn historically indeterminate and a continuous present. An astute introduction by the magazine's editor, Elizabeth Gordon, framed the concept of *shibui* as a figurative ideal that could be embraced by western culture, and by North American culture in particular, as the antidote to the industrialized design of the modern movement. Adopting a flexible approach to history, she claimed to see in the classical Japanese tradition a concept that was clearly antithetical to mechanistic thinking, to the Bauhaus and the international style of architecture, with *shibui* standing for "organic simplicity producing richness. It is not negation and austerity for it is developed to the hilt."

Gordon's assessment betrays the typical guilt complex provoked by the "indifferent design" dominating American production, a complex that Americans are trying to rid themselves of by looking to distant cultures for new ideas that can be absorbed into academic and eclectic syntheses. But what interests us here is Gordon's view of the ongoing development of Japanese architecture. She argues that the age of *shibui* may be coming to an end, as vulgar western forms inundate the country, with only traces of the thousand-year tradition remaining in the form of artifacts, poems, music, and gardens. Glad therefore to have witnessed *shibui* in everyday life, she hopes that perhaps America can adopt it before it disappears from Japan altogether, just as it has assimilated and Americanized other foreign concepts.

Leading Japanese critics responded decisively to Gordon's call for an indiscriminate return to *shibui*, with its implied criticism of contemporary Japanese architecture, describing the situation with a historical maturity unmatched by the American critics.[63] The rebuke, mild at first in the contributions of the art critic Michiaki Kawakita and of Yoshiro Taniguchi in *Gegutsu Shuncho*, would become more strident, with Yuchiro Kojirō writing in *Japan Architect*:[64]

> I suspect that the reason for the success of *shibui* in America is that Americans, possessing as they do an extremely high standard of living, are seeking to find a deeper richness than that which comes from superficial brightness. To us, however, *shibui* is a concept born of the attempt on the part of the urban commoners of old, prevented by aristocratic oppression from living luxuriously, to find a sort of concealed richness. *Shibui* implies, among other things, a protest against the luxurious beauty of aristocratic life. It is deeply connected with the cult of tea, which was also created by the oppressed townsmen of the past. Perhaps it can add to the depth of culture in America, where people are well off, but in Japan we cannot ignore the inhumanity and subservience intrinsic in its historical origin.[65]

The terms of the Japanese critics' argument show their engagement with a cultural process of historicizing and evaluating events in Japan in the most authentic way, without any myth-making, but with an eye also on contemporary global developments. In

---

63  *Architectural Record* would follow up with its own impassioned article on the concept in April 1961.
64  Yūichirō Kōjirō, "View of Japanese Architecture," *Japan Architect*, September 1961. This issue also includes an article by Bruno Zevi summarizing the debate, first published in Italy ("Vanno in Giappone per dimenticare Le Corbusier," *L'Espresso,* March 5, 1961) and an article by Charles Terry, "Taking Exception."
65  Kojirō, "View of Japanese Architecture," 68.

one sense a continuation of the critical reassessment of Japanese culture that began at the end of the nineteenth century, with the studies by K. Kigo, C. Ito, and T. Sekino, this process has absorbed architecture's break with the past and now brings to it a capacity for critical thinking that can guide future developments.[66]

It is also significant that the first international editions of Japanese architectural journals appeared around 1956/57 (*Shinkenchiku*, followed by *Japan Architect*, *Japan Design*, etc.), a sign of the growing awareness of the specific role of Japanese architecture within the modern movement. In the extremely high standard of the architecture produced in recent years, we see ample confirmation of that now defining role.

The current architectural scene of the 1960s is dominated by a series of young designers who have enthusiastically embraced the innovations of the masters of the new school—when they have not played a direct role in those innovations themselves. Having already referred to the importance of Masato Ōtaka within Maekawa's MID group, we will now briefly analyze the work of Kiyonori Kikutake, who along with Ōtaka is arguably the most forward-thinking of the new generation. As we will see below, Kikutake and Ōtaka have collaborated closely on the urban megastructure projects of the Metabolist group.

Before that, however, Kikutake had already gained a certain notoriety as the driving force of a group of students from the Waseda School of Architecture who became internationally famous when they won prizes at the São Paulo Biennial for three years running. Kikutake would come third in the competition for the Hiroshima Peace Memorial Park, behind Tange,

---

[66] This mature critical discourse based on profound historical thinking can be followed in Japanese publications over recent years, especially in journals of modern architecture. In addition to frequent critical analyses of historic buildings, there are incisive overviews which consider how radical architects can historicize their work. Among the most interesting articles are: Gakuji Yamamoto, "The Development of Contemporary Architecture and the Consciousness of Tradition," *Shinkenchiku*, no. 7 (1956); Hirotaro Ōta, "A Historical Comment on Japanese-Style Architecture as Visual Language," *Shinkenchiku*, no. 8 (1956); and Kiyoshi Higuchi, "Restore Man and Nature to Architecture," *Japan Architect*, February–March 1961.

Fig. 82 Kiyonori Kikutake, Apartments in Tonogaya

and after spells working in the office of Murano and Mori (1951) and in the research group of Motowo Take at the University of Waseda (from 1952)[67] he would open his own practice in 1957 and realize apartment buildings at Kunitachi and Tonogaya (fig. 82).[68] The highly expressive language of those buildings—a blend of the poetics of *béton brut* with an aggressive massing and an accentuated play of light and shadow—is reiterated in the Shimane Prefecture Museum at Matsue (1960), where the elementary geometric figure of the upper volume rises sharply from a base characterized by a rigorous, chiaroscuro

---

67  Motowo Take, a professor at the University of Waseda, has exerted a strong influence on young Japanese architects, much more for his teaching than for his scant, not particularly interesting built work. His most recent projects, also inspired by Corbusian Brutalism, include the Sports Center at the University of Waseda and the Nagasaki Aquarium, begun in 1959.

68  The typology adopted in the Tonogaya Apartment Building is very interesting. Like Maekawa's Harumi Apartments, the interiors based on traditional tatami mats are set in a structural grid where the functional cores of the central services and stairs shown in the plan and elevations correspond on the exterior to windowless, exposed reinforced concrete walls. See *Shinkenchiku*, January 1957: 27–34.

fragmentation, introducing a note of drama into the measured, balanced composition (figs. 83 and 84). This dramatic element becomes more pronounced in recent works such as the Hitotsubashi Middle School Gymnasium in Tokyo (1961)—and even more so in the project for the new Izumo Shrine Administrative Building, now under construction, which overtly signals a violent break with the past, a rare occurrence in the extremely conservative realm of Japanese religious architecture.

Another young architect in the Metabolist group with similar interests to Kikutake is Fumihiko Maki. Of his generation, he is the one with the most extensive international experience. After completing his degree at Tokyo University, he pursued graduate studies at Cranbrook Academy of Art and Harvard Graduate School of Design. He worked in turn in the offices of Skidmore, Owings and Merrill, Josep Lluís Sert, and Kenzō Tange. His varied architectural training is reflected in his slightly eclectic approach (see, for example, his most important building to date, the auditorium of the University of Nagoya), which is tempered, however, by the originality of his treatment of the construction and its elements.

Maki recently presented a project for the redevelopment of the center of the Dōjima district in Osaka in collaboration with the architectural department of the Takenaka Corporation.[69] Clearly inspired by North American urban renewal projects, the design proposes to turn the whole central area into a self-contained pedestrian zone ringed by elevated highways connected to the main urban and regional traffic arteries (figs. 85 and 86). Thus, rather than attempting an integration of the area into the existing fabric of the city, the intervention proposes a rupture, carving out a tidy, uniform island from the chaotic mix of speculative high-rises and traditional low-rise construction that defines the urban character of Osaka (and other large Japanese cities). One of the more interesting elements of Maki's design is his development of the system of modular "functional cores" that contain

---

69  See *Japan Architect*, June 1962: 10–54.

Fig. 83 Kiyonori Kikutake, Shimane Prefecture Museum

Fig. 84 Kiyonori Kikutake, Shimane Prefecture Museum

POSTWAR ARCHITECTURE

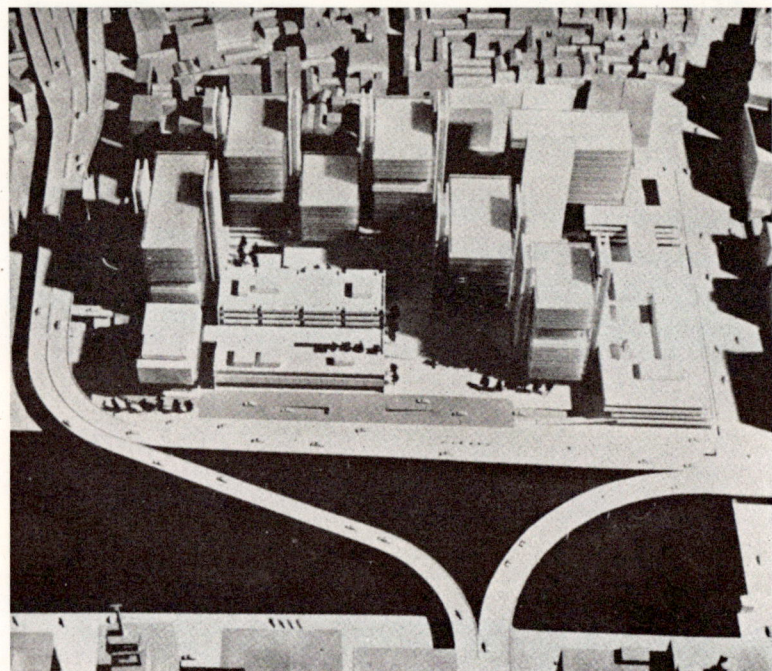

Fig. 85
Fumihiko
Maki, Dōjima
Redevelopment
Plan, Osaka

Fig. 86
Fumihiko
Maki, Dōjima
Redevelopment
Plan, Osaka

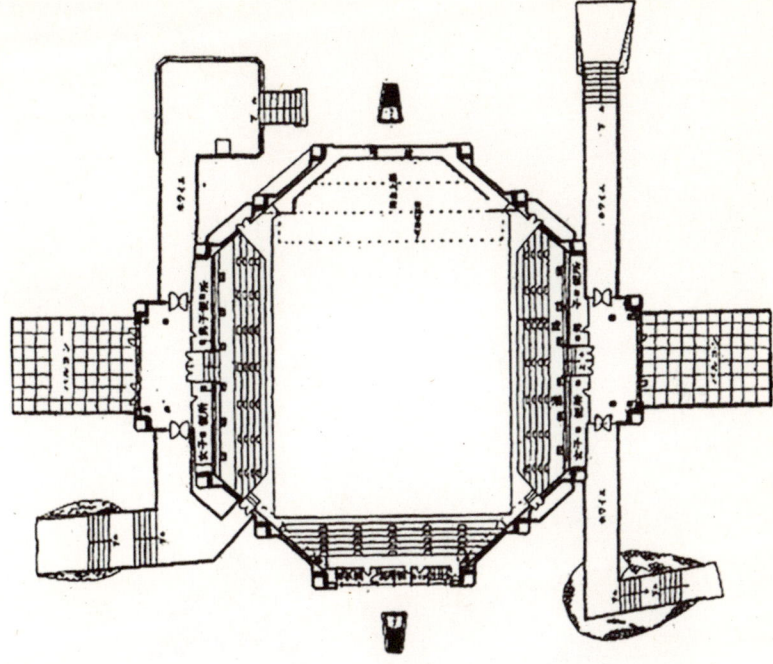

Fig. 87
Eiji Miyagawa,
Niigata
Prefectural
Gymnasium

the load-bearing structure and services of the office buildings. While it takes its cue from the system Tange introduced in his plan for Tokyo, its spirit and scale are different, in that it also provides a fixed framework of reference for defining the complex's relations to the urban surroundings—relations that are uncoupled from an overall vision of the city, to be sure, but the method has some positive aspects that are further specified and elaborated in the second draft of the plan (1962).

Another significant recent work is Eiji Miyagawa's Niigata Prefectural Gymnasium (figs. 87 and 88), which achieves a synthesis of pure structure and highly emotive plasticity. Again the structure is overstated for expressive purposes, but in the process it gains an unprecedented coherence and dramatic intensity. The structural principle that defines the roof—a hyperbolic-paraboloid shell anchored by two structural ties—is not original.

Fig. 88
Eiji Miyagawa,
Niigata
Prefectural
Gymnasium

Tange, among others, had already used it to great effect in the Shizuoka Convention Hall. But what those earlier examples lack is the exceptional figural tension, the insolence of the expansive but tightly controlled composition, the almost provocative effect of the elements that are deliberately designed to be aggressive, rough—even unpleasant in the case of some of the joints—for precise polemical reasons.

Noting some inconsistencies within the structural organization, the critic Gen Kawakami observed:

> I do not wish to attack this point, however, because I am not a member of the cult which holds that structural truth is identical with structural beauty. In my opinion, people regard a structure as beautiful when their experience or their unconscious theoretical knowledge tells them that it is strong—strong enough to withstand the elements and to continue to live throughout the ages. In a public building of this sort, it is desirable that people be given something that pleases them visually, something that appears strong and vital, and for that reason there is no need to stick dogmatically to the calculations that a strictly physical consideration would yield.[70]

Kawakami's critique, ingenuously formulated as it may be, points to a way of going beyond the purely technical approaches that remain so fashionable on the international scene.

A revisiting of the expressive violence of concrete structures and "brutal" surfaces can also be seen in the most recent works of Murano and Mori, and in particular the Yonago Public Hall—severe and dramatic with no concession to formal niceties—and the Yokohama City Hall, with its forthright display of the structural grid. All are of a high architectural standard, even if a certain staleness can be detected in the latter work especially.

---

[70] Gen Kawakami, "Gymnasium Design and the HP-Shell," *Japan Architect*, February 1961: 38.

Alongside these enthusiastic young innovators, it is possible to identify two other currents on the Japanese scene, although the word "currents" is only really useful as a didactic device, a shorthand way of labelling styles that appear to be related but do not share a consciously defined cultural strategy. On the one hand, there are the architects who remain faithful to the language and methodology of rationalism in the strictest sense. In this group we can include not only some of the older masters from the prewar period, such as Mamoru Yamada, Sutemi Horiguchi, or Hiroshi Ōe, but also a large number of younger architects, some of whose work from the 1950s we have already looked at. However, it should be noted that the profound rupture provoked by the new school has visibly affected both the formal choices and the design methods of these neo-rationalist architects. Surveying Japanese rationalism over the last four or five years, we see a language that is more critically mature than in the 1952–56 period, and often enhanced by brutalist-style modulations.

On the other hand, there are the architects and large professional organizations that make extensive use of the curtain wall, giving rise to huge complexes that have the inert, nondescript appearance typical of architecture that is the sole product of industrialized construction, uninflected by cultural or aesthetic aims.

Among the architects in the former group, we could single out Masachika Murata, one of the "in-between generation" who has devoted most of his career to the design of community buildings. Worthy of note are his Aichi Country Club (1954), which is lent a certain formalism by the adaptation of the plan to the uneven terrain, and, even more, the large municipal swimming pool at Sendagaya in Tokyo (1958).

Murata's first hall for the International Trade Fair Buildings in Tokyo (fig. 89), completed in 1959, manages successfully to combine a restatement of the traditional modulation of the building envelope with a sober display of structuralism: the vast roof of the main pavilion is supported by a series of inverted V-shaped

Fig. 89
Masachika Murata,
Shopping Center, Tokyo

reinforced concrete columns that effectively dematerialize the perimeter of the building, drawing the eye to the pattern of the curtain wall, which has something of the modular purism of classical Japanese works from the Momoyama or Edo periods. Less successful is his second exhibition hall, designed in collaboration with the engineer Yoshikatsu Tsuboi, a Nervi-inspired vaulted structure that fails to go beyond pure structural display.

In Komazawa Park in Tokyo, Ashihara and Murata are realizing sports facilities for the 1964 Olympic Games within the framework of a masterplan devised by the Takayama Institute at the University of Tokyo. Preparations for the Olympics also include, among other things, the construction of an entire network of roads to connect the various sports facilities across the city. However, this network appears to be imposed without reference to wider considerations, with no attempt being made to integrate it organically into an overall urban plan.[71]

The project for Komazawa Park envisions a gymnasium and a large stadium standing like isolated objects—formal opposites—within a vast campus. Judging from the available models and drawings, Murata's stadium displays a sound understanding,

---

71   As in Rome in 1960, the Tokyo Olympics have benefited speculators, as various Japanese critics have pointed out, but they have also provided the opportunity to build large-scale structures and infrastructures.

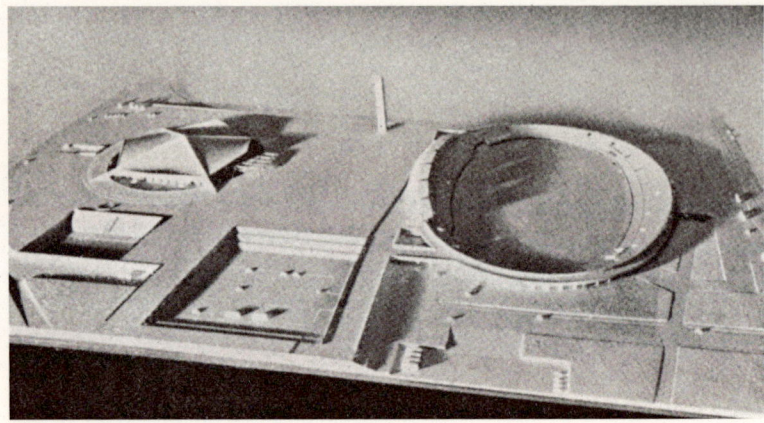

Fig. 90 Masachika Murata and Yoshinobu Ashihara, Olympic Facilities

and expressive use, of the potential of the structure, whereas Ashihara's gymnasium is defined by a belabored structuralism that suggests a staleness, not just in the work of the architect, but in a whole methodology that aims at objectivity but readily lapses into overstatement and rhetoric when it strives for more complex effects (fig. 90).[72]

A similar staleness can be found among other brave souls working in the rationalist tradition when they resort to structuralism as a means of extracting themselves from their own personal *impasse*. Their approach, then, is quite different from that of the young brutalists, for whom the amplification of the expressiveness of the architectural image goes hand in hand with the glorification of the structure, as two aspects of the same creative process. Viewed from this perspective, the works of Tomoya Masuda (to give a particularly illuminating example)—and in particular the pump room in the Toba water treatment plant in Kyoto or the as yet unrealized project for a new airport for the same city—bespeak a substantial cultural void that cannot be covered up by an insistent use of unitary structural forms.

---

[72] In some of his more recent works, including the Kagawa Prefectural Library, Ashihara seems to have adopted brutalist poetics in contrast with to his usual preference for smooth, clear-cut volumes.

The best designers still manage to avoid this rationalist regression, however, by continually refining their language, at times adopting avant-garde tones in the process. Among them is Antonin Raymond, a vocal supporter, as mentioned above, of Maekawa's Tokyo Festival Hall. In the Gunma Music Center in Takasaki (1961), Raymond adopts an expressiveness of materials and structure without abandoning his own constructionist approach. Similarly, in the auditorium for the Tōyō Eiwa Girls School (fig. 91), Hiroshi Ōe draws closer to the style of the new school while maintaining his focus on the elementary, expressed here at the level of construction: a series of massive pillars support two main hollow beams, the ovoid section of which is prominently displayed on the exterior. As a whole, the building is defined by a limpidity far removed from the highly wrought expressiveness of the brutalist current.

It appears significant that Ōe and many others in the same rationalist strand have absorbed the methods and syntax typical of the new school. In the past few years, generally, the formal language of Japanese architecture has displayed a notable homogeneity, reflecting the strong inspiration of the work of Tange, Maekawa, and Sakakura. Their new ways of articulating and deploying the latest technology are finding resonance even with architects who remain culturally distant from the experimentation of the new school.

Interestingly, the galvanizing effect of the architectural innovators extends even to the large corporate practices that have taken that root in Japan in response to the ever-increasing scale of production, and are in a certain sense creating monopolies in building construction. Some of these giant corporations rival their North American equivalents in terms of their size and work organization. Nikken, based in Osaka, but with offices in Tokyo, Nagoya, and Fukuoka, now has as many employees as Skidmore, Owings, and Merrill, while Mitsubishi has a similar set up. These huge organizations control around one third of architectural production, another third is realized by private practices, while the remaining third is in the hands of government offices or the

Fig. 91
Hiroshi Ōe,
Tōyō Eiwa Girls
School

Fig. 92
Hideo Kosaka,
Kyoto Post
Office and
Savings Bank

architecture departments of prefectures and municipalities. Particularly interesting, in this last category, is the high standard of the work of the architecture department of the Ministry of Posts and Telegraphs under the direction of Hideo Kosaka. But we should also note a reversal of the American phenomenon in Japan: here, it is not the large corporate offices but rather the projects of the new school that lead the way in terms of style and working methods, exerting a profound influence even on organizations with close ties to big capital.

Kyoto Post Office and Savings Bank (1954), set within a medieval garden, typifies Hideo Kosaka's approach (fig. 92). Here, the purely rationalist glazed volume enters into a dialogue with the symbolic naturalism of the exceptional existing environment, achieving a formal balance defined by a rare sensibility. Other works by Kosaka, such as the Aichi Prefectural Cultural Center or the Post Office Headquarters at Nagoya, evince the same kind of balance. Confronted with this perfect symbiosis of modern working methods and classical spirit, we are tempted to argue that his approach is somewhat escapist, particularly in relation to the dramatic restatement of history and tradition pursued by Tange and Maekawa.

The recent output of the Nikken architectural office is also interesting, though it is hardly characterized by a collective style—on the contrary, the internal structuring and the size of the company are more conducive to a personalization of individual projects, meaning there is little continuity between the various works. Thus, in the excellent library for the Japanese Chemical Association in Tokyo, the restrained expressiveness of the exposed structure and the vigorous detailing suggest an original reinterpretation of Sakakura's style, whereas the library for Otsuma High School, near the Imperial Palace of Tokyo, seems to show the influence of Murano (fig. 93). In turn, the clubhouse for the staff of the Tokai Bank in Nagoya and, even more, the Nippon Sheet Glass Company Offices (fig. 94), refer to a more conformist, Americanized conception of the International Style.[73]

Fig. 93
Studio Nikken, Otsuma High School, library

Fig. 94
Studio Nikken, Office Building for Nippon Sheet Glass Co.

But "indifferent rationalism" is becoming less common on the Japanese scene and appears—at least to those observing from a distance—to be a phenomenon on the wane, with no prospects for further development. The initiative is now firmly in the hands of the younger generations who, in their recent projects especially, have shown a growing commitment to the problem of the city and the new dimension of social relations. This is a topic that requires its own detailed treatment. A number of general observations, however, may serve to introduce the current discourse on Japanese *urban utopias*.

The great vitality of modern Japanese architecture has an undoubted flipside in the form of the structural shortcomings of economic and urban planning. Japanese architects today have to choose between two basic categories of clients: private capital and public authorities. The new school has made the clear choice to concentrate its energies on the public sector, to make civic buildings that stand as symbols of new social structures and new urban relations—buildings defined by a heightened expressiveness that

---

73   The Nippon Sheet Glass Company Offices are clearly designed to highlight their product for advertising purposes. This approach is also found in other buildings designed by the corporate studios.

is often defiant, but always intended to point out an alternative way. Their works are designed for the entire population, who are conceived as the protagonists of the architecture, rather than as *passive consumers*—the role to which they have been relegated by the mechanisms of neo-capitalist production.

However, it is no coincidence that our analyses have invariably turned up isolated "pieces" that fall outside any city plan or unitary development. As with many other phenomena in Japan's current socio-political system, the contradictions here take on an extreme character: alongside the richness and bold expressiveness of Japanese architecture, there is an almost total lack of planning that deprives that architecture of its most effective, crucial premise. In this context, the glorification of the structure, the brutalism, and the aggressive plasticity of so many works in recent years might be explained as an attempt to compensate for these shortcomings, if not as a symbolic protest. Forced to produce isolated pieces of architecture, quasi-monuments, in an increasingly disordered and irrational urban fabric, architects have responded by accentuating the enforced character of rupture and isolation (Maekawa's Harumi Apartments come to mind) in a process that shares some similarities with the strategies adopted by Brazilian architects.[74]

Brutalism now appears to be a kind of self-defense mechanism for modern Japanese architecture—a defense that is at the same time an attack, drawing from this dual character an ethical rationale that compensates for the inevitable imbalances and allows us to pardon, or at least to justify, the excesses and the crises that we have explored here.

74     "The formal agitation [in Brazil] was undoubtedly determined partly by a defensive attitude towards the dense and chaotic urban surroundings ... Formalism arose, as in Scandinavia, in the presence of very particular social pattern—in Scandinavia, of a socially very equal society and an economy based on co-operation, in Brazil, of a hierarchical society and recently born but flourishing capitalism—which for this reason demanded appropriate symbolic representation." Benevolo, *History of Modern Architecture*, vol. 2, 754–55.

# IV  JAPANESE URBAN PLANNING

## 1. Urban reality and the Tokyo general zoning plan

Urbanism is treated separately from architecture here because of the singularity of Japanese experience in this area. We have already mentioned the imbalances resulting from a lack of economic and urban planning in the country, a typical feature of societies embarking on the path of modern capitalism. In the immediate aftermath of the war, a political antipathy to planning appeared to counter that capitalist expansion. The need for planning, for coordinated programs, only became part of the Japanese political mindset later on, when the country reached an advanced stage of economic development. Even then, in Japan, urban planning was treated in isolation, and not as part of a national plan.[75]

But for foreign observers it is particularly interesting to see how the liveliest elements of Japanese architectural culture have responded to the general pattern of urban development—to a chaotic situation that, in terms of its scale and particular characteristics, is only partially relatable to the chaos of European cities, and perhaps even American ones too. The renewed international interest in Japan in recent years, then, is not solely about the lessons that can be directly absorbed from its built architecture; it is also concerned with a series of visionary "urban utopias" and their response to the challenges posed by the modern metropolis and new ways of living.

And so we come to a familiar dichotomy. Planning, in the sense of an organic synthesis of economic and spatial interventions, is either completely lacking in Japan, or found only in a sector-based form (with no vertical or horizontal integration between urban plan and economic policy, say, or between individual zones and the wider territory). And yet this same context is the seedbed for proposals for new urban structures that attempt to go beyond the limits imposed by the current political and social reality.

Expressed in graphically powerful images, the urban utopias of Tange and the younger groups are both a reaction to and a denunciation of that situation. But their influence on the international scene would be limited if they were nothing more than elaborate forms of protest. Instead, if we strip away the unrealistic and deliberately polemical aspects of these futuristic visions, we can extract some ideas that are relevant to the modern movement as a whole. Underlying the exaggeration of these utopias, their desperate search for a "new dimension" by which to order urban space and human settlements, is an impulse that should not be overlooked, and that could serve as a warning to the

---

75  See "Town Planning in Evolution," in Richards, *An Architectural Journey*, 117–18, and Manabu Tajima, "I quattro periodi dell'urbanistica giapponese," *Casabella continuità*, no. 273 (1963): 16–29.

modern movement, reminding it of its commitment to defining the elements of the "new city"—elements that up to now have constantly eluded the control of architects and of culture in general, being shaped instead by the rapid growth of capitalist society, or, in the case of countries with popular democracies, by a fashion for self-imposed limits on culture.

A reordering of the whole society—that seems to be the thrust of these proposals for new urban structures. But does this not pose the risk of regressing into the same (spent) illusions that drove the "revolution of the technocrats"? And even if these architects were to limit their actions to their own field—that is, to the ordering of space—is there not a danger that the vast dimensions of the proposed buildings would impoverish the content of the architecture?

The young Japanese architects do not appear to have explicitly considered these legitimate questions, even though they should form the starting point, the first hypothesis to be tested in reality. Even Tange, who has undertaken a serious study of the development of the contemporary metropolis, does not engage with the broader discourse that the scope of his projects inevitably implies.

To assess the significance of the young Japanese architects' proposals, we need first to form an overview of the planning and legislative structures in the center of decision-making in the country, Tokyo. Only in this city has there been an attempt to draw up a coordinated program of interventions, although the result, as we will see, is very much open to criticism.

1956 saw the enactment of the first plan for the structuring of the whole of the vast region connected to the capital. Marking the beginning of a policy of decentralization, it was conceived to prevent any further concentration of housing or industrial facilities in the central urban area, with the aim of preventing further road congestion, even if only temporarily.[76] As a result

---

76    See "Situazione e prospettive della città di Tokyo," *Informazioni urbanistiche*, nos. 3–4 (1961): 34–45.

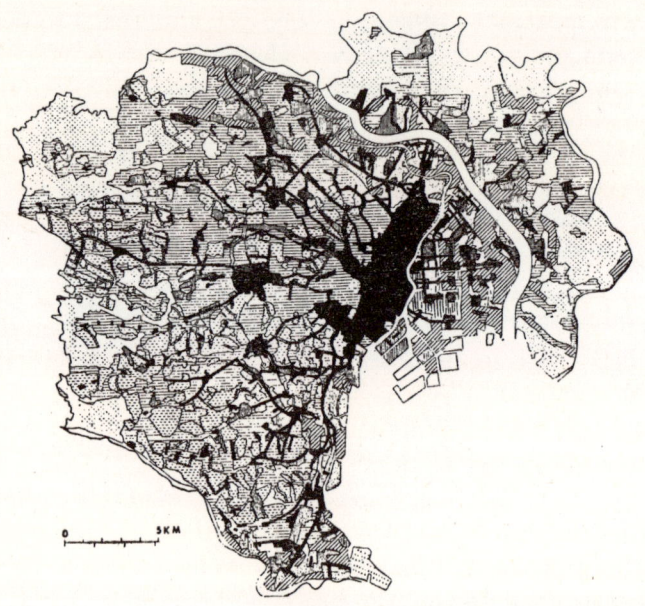

Fig. 95
Tokyo Zoning

of this plan, the city and the surrounding region have become more closely tied and interdependent. The plan is divided into three distinct zones according to function: an *urban zone*, a *green belt*, and a *peripheral zone*. In the *urban zone*, high-density construction is permitted within a radius of 50km around the central station: almost all of this is allocated for housing, with specific limits and controls being placed on the development of new industrial areas. In the *green belt*, which extends for 10km beyond the urban zone, no new residential construction is permitted; existing residential areas are being reduced in size and reconfigured as satellite towns. Finally, the *peripheral zone*, which extends beyond the green belt to a maximum distance of around 100km from the central station, is to support new satellite towns (figs. 95 and 96) equipped with autonomous services and adequate production facilities, as part of an evident attempt to achieve a rational decentralization of the city as a whole.[77] The implementation of this vast program has been

Fig. 96
Regional scheme of the Tokyo plan

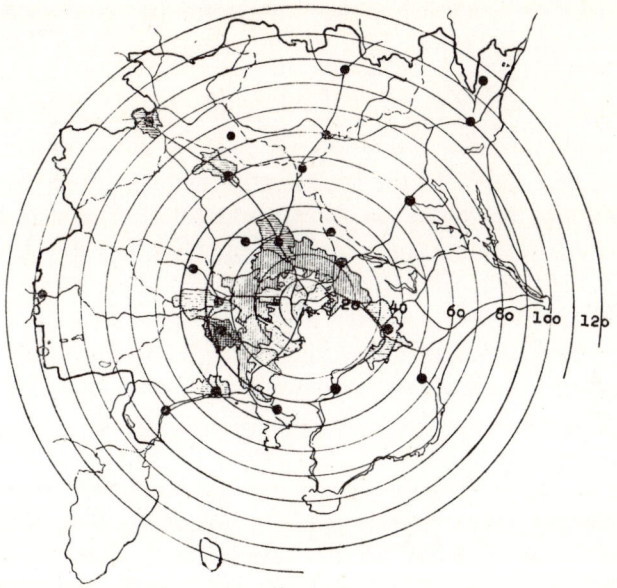

entrusted to a "commission for the development of the region of the national capital" appointed by the government to draft and refine the regional plan. The plan, in turn, is made up of a regional general plan and individual construction programs: the former establishes policy guidelines that are valid for an indefinite period, while the latter are valid for ten years and are instituted on an annual basis in line with the allocation of government funding determined by the regional development law.

This regional law is supplemented by two special measures: a law for the development of urbanized zones, enacted in 1958, regulates the creation of new satellite towns, specifying the financing mechanisms, while a second law, approved the

77  The largest of these satellite towns, Hino, some 40km from the Tokyo, is designed for a population of 30,000. It is now the base for a number of manufacturing firms that relocated from the capital in with policy of industrial decentralization begun in 1957. The new town, with its mass housing for industrial workers, has largely been constructed by the largest Japanese developer, the Japan Housing Corporation. See *Informazioni urbanistiche*, nos. 3–4 (1961): 44.

JAPANESE URBAN PLANNING

following year, establishes the criteria for the construction of new factories and public facilities in both the old and the newly built residential zones.[78]

Rather than dwelling on the shortcomings of the provisions, it is more interesting to look at the cultural aspects that have shaped them. Here, we see an obvious affinity between the solutions proposed for Tokyo and those tried out in the famous Abercrombie and Forshaw plan for Greater London. Alongside the typical Anglo-Saxon concept of decentralization, there is an attempt to control the economic and urban development of a metropolis that had reached unsustainable levels of density through a series of external measures aimed at rebalancing the whole system. In its application to Japan, however, we find a completely uncritical acceptance of an approach that—even if it had become a cornerstone of the history of modern city planning—was already partly obsolete in 1956, when the general zoning plan for Tokyo was published.

Tange's criticism of the passive translation into Japanese of an experiment rooted in a very different historical context is particularly incisive: "Our administration"—he wrote—"only contemplates the reconstruction, the reorganization after the catastrophe. It fails to see the need to prevent new catastrophes by means of new building programs."[79]

---

[78] In Japan there is no real building program even for public housing. There are, however, four types of housing built with state funds or subsidies: a) housing built only with state funds; b) housing built by local governments with a fifty percent state contribution divided into two categories (for middle-income classes and minimum-income classes; the former category are assigned by a lottery of vetted applications); c) housing built by the Japan Housing Corporation with mixed public and private capital; d) housing built by the Housing Loan Corporation, favoring families with mortgages at a low interest rate, underwritten by the state. See, also, *Informazioni urbanistiche*, nos. 3–4 (1961): 40, and the following articles in *Shinkenchiku*, no. 9 (1956): Jirō Hayashida, "Comments on the Housing Financing Corporation's Houses"; Motoo Miyazaki, "Character of Housing Financing Corporation"; Ryuichi Hamaguchi, "Image of a Family as Reflected in Room Arrangement"; Fumo Hayakawa, "Popular Choices in House Plans."

[79] Quoted in Kultermann, *Architecture nouvelle,* 14. In 1961, however, the government accepted the proposal to create an urban planning faculty at the University of Tokyo that had been put forward by the Japanese Association of Architects in 1960. Indeed, 1960 can be considered a key year for the revival of Japanese urban planning: in May, the Metabolist group presented their utopias at the World Design Conference in Tokyo, and, shortly afterwards, Tange published his Plan for Tokyo.

## 2. The Metabolists and the Neo-Mastaba group

The construction of satellite towns, the incentives for industrial decentralization, and the further legislative provisions have had minimal impact on the chaotic situation of the Japanese capital. The ineffectiveness of the official plans, combined with the rapid growth of Tokyo and the obvious shortcomings in its urban structure, provide the context for the creation of a series of utopian proposals for the solution of the city's problems, which are of a magnitude that more or less legitimizes the positing of a utopia.

A high degree of utopianism characterizes the urban research of the Metabolist movement (the name is intended to symbolize its vision of society as a living being in a continuous process of development). Its founding members, in addition to Kikutake, Ōtaka, and Maki, who have been mentioned above, include the architect Noriaki "Kishō" Kurokawa and the young critic Noboru Kawazoe.

> When a society has assimilated an architectural technique, architects must compare this technique with their own conceptions. Techniques do not have social reality insofar as they come from constructions; the words that describe them with their primitive technical, physical or functional meanings become slogans that basically stem from social phenomena.[80]

These words appear in a little publication from 1960 that documents the urban research of the young Metabolists. The theoretical explanations that accompany the presentation of the projects, though at times repetitive, are extremely interesting as evidence of a mood and a significant achievement in contemporary Japanese culture.[81]

---

80  Noriaki Kurokawa, "Propositions d'urbanisme au Japon," *Architecture d'aujourd'hui*, no. 101 (1962): 84.

When the president of the Japanese Housing Corporation, Kyuro Kano, proposed a polder-like infill of the east side of Tokyo Bay, to gain land to build a satellite town without the complications of real-estate speculation, young architects responded with even more ambitious projects of their own. Ōtaka put his buildings directly on the water. This approach, he said, would cost half as much as the land reclamation: there was no need for a complicated system of dykes when the piers could be sunk directly in the seabed. An even bolder proposal by Kikutake pushed to the limit the idea of expanding into the water. He envisioned the construction of gigantic, floating reinforced-concrete rafts to house a city of 3,000 inhabitants, with residential towers, public parks, airdromes, etc. Each residential node was to be directly linked to Tokyo by means of ferries (fig. 97). Kurokawa took a different approach, suspending a new fabric of housing above the existing city center.

Among the more interesting projects in the 1960 book are Kurokawa's Agricultural City, a horizontal grid-like structure integrating housing and all collective services and infrastructure (fig. 98), and the Shinjuku Subcenter project by Ōtaka and Maki, which distills their innovative research into a series of standard models for didactic purposes (fig. 99).[82]

What all these projects share is an attempt to introduce a larger urban scale—one that allows for greater freedom and

[81] Kiyonori Kikutake, Noboru Kawazoe, Masato Ōtaka and Fumihiko Maki, and Noriaki Kurokawa, *Metabolism 1960: The Proposals for New Urbanism* (Tokyo: 1960). "Our conception of the city of the future"—writes Kawazoe—"must be one which embraces disorder, which finds a new order within this disorder, and which in fact is capable of building a new order out of confusion … Even if we actually do propose some such total image, we do not mean to advocate that our ideas must be realized exactly as they are… Our proposals are nothing more than mere segments of an image, or else mere suggestions about the directions and the methods to be taken … Let us have countless new Utopias; and let there be endless proposals, so that we may have mutual stimulation and attain a progressive enrichment and clarification … The city of the future must be a state of unity of Art and the advances of the masses. Naturally, the free, spontaneous energies of the masses must be given effective play in the construction of the city. Since the above-mentioned 'architecture reduced to parts' will be subject to any combination according to the free will of the masses, the appearance of the city will not be an orderly one at all, in other words, not a fixed one as heretofore." Noboru Kawazoe, "The City of the Future," *Zodiac*, no. 9 (1962): 99–101.

[82] See Kikutake et al., *Metabolism 1960*, and Kawazoe, "The City of the Future."

Fig. 97
Kiyonori
Kikutake,
Ocean City

Fig. 98
Kisho Kurokawa,
Agricultural
City

JAPANESE URBAN PLANNING

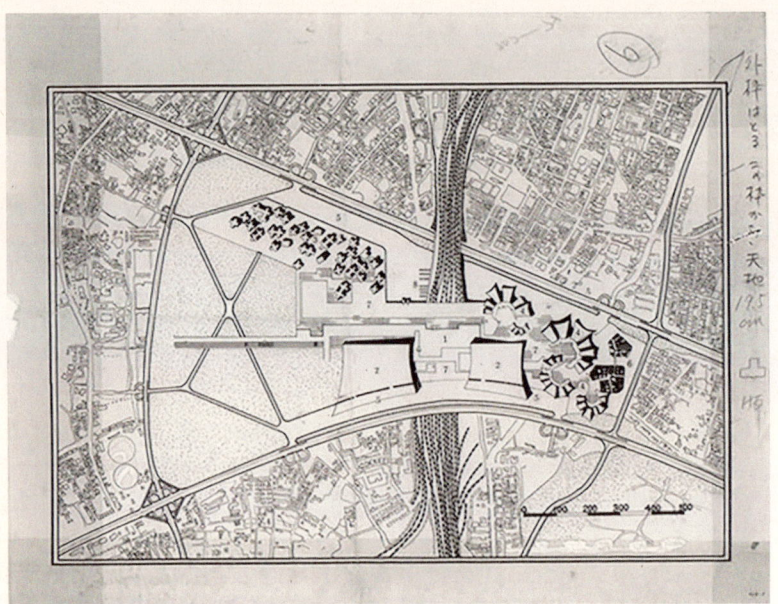

Fig. 99
Fumihiko Maki and Masato Otaka, Shinjuku Subcenter

continual adaptation over time—and an interest in a new naturalism associated with an often naive social utopianism, in which the ideas of Le Corbusier are exalted to the point of paroxysm. This, for example, is how Kikutake describes his model of a mobile housing unit:

> The large parts-pieces of the housing unit will be assembled in the factory near the tower and after careful checking will be placed with their base along an assembly ring, from here raised to the sky and lastly anchored to their established position. Like a warm wish for a new family unit about to be born, the new dwelling will take its place up there in the sky. People living in the tower and all around will be able to send their fervid wishes to the new couple, and the new family will welcome with joy not only their new dwelling but also their elevation toward the sky, which symbolizes their taking their place as members of urban society.[83]

Although the formulation of their projects and the emphasis of their theoretical explanations speak of a sincere, enthusiastic search for new kinds of solutions, the young Metabolists remain mired in a generic avant-gardism, treating the great problems that confront humanity and society in such an abstract and metaphorical way that their methods lose any potential for development and, with this, diminish the incisive, mordant quality of their utopianism as well.

Among the numerous other utopian projects for "future cities" developed by young Japanese architects, the work of the Neo-Mastaba group, though not as stimulating or suggestive for practice, is nonetheless interesting on account of their proposed restructuring of the city, in which the various urban functions are condensed in pyramid structures where the floors are connected to each other by rack elevators that operate at a 45-degree angle, along the load-bearing structure.

But this takes us into a *utopia for utopia's sake*, one which appears to be not so far removed from a new kind of academicism that treats research as an end in itself, rather than as a means to break with the past and move toward a new constructivity. This limitation can be found in every avant-garde movement, but it is particularly evident in those of Japan, in all areas of the arts.

83 See Kikutake et al., *Metabolism 1960*. Kikutake's project was illustrated by Tange at CIAM Otterlo in 1959. See J. Joedicke, ed., *Dokumente der modernen Architektur* (Stuttgart: Karl Krämer, 1961), 184–85.

## 3. Tange's plans for Boston and Tokyo

a) *The MIT Plan for Boston.* In one sense all of the projects we have briefly surveyed either anticipate, or follow on from, the Plan for Tokyo by Kenzō Tange. Tange's international renown led him to be invited to teach at the Massachusetts Institute of Technology (where Pietro Belluschi was chair of urban planning). It was his experience at MIT, where he was visiting professor of urbanism from September 1959 to February 1960, that furnished the methodological premise of his Tokyo Plan.

The theme of the assignment that Tange set his fifth-year students—a new settlement for 25,000 people in Boston Bay—was chosen as a means to analyze the contradictions and confusion provoked by the rapid transformation of society in our modern world; a transformation we are no longer able to control with the tools currently at our disposal. For Tange, technology is not inevitably and irredeemably incompatible with the need to humanize the technocratic world: on the contrary, he sees the reconciliation of these two things as the main task of the modern architect. "But to achieve this our current methods and terminology are ineffectual," he writes:

> We need to create a new model of urban settlement. The house, street, and quarter, these different levels of community are the elements making up the city. Each element must have a certain degree of unity and perfection but at the same time be open toward the superior level to create a larger scale entity. We must consider the need to preserve identity at each level and at the same time we must make comprehensible and accessible the importance and significance of each individual element within the general system ... As for treating the problem of the links between the various functions of society, modern means of transport introduce new possibilities: highways. The superhuman scale of the highway is not uniform with existing architectural

forms but naturally this does not mean that the superhuman scale must be rejected.[84]

The problem is therefore to define a single urban organism that not only has the necessary scale to accommodate modern means of communication, but also responds to the need to humanize the new technologies. It could be distilled as an attempt to imbue the alienating technology of neo-capitalist society with an authentically social dimension.

There is also, however, a powerful, rationalist-type component to this approach. Here, the spatial and expressive dimensions of the city are called on to resolve social issues and conflict, as if the structures and behavior of society could be regulated through the physical structure of the city.

This residual constructivist approach makes Tange's ideas somewhat abstract (though much less so than those of the young utopians we have just looked at). That said, his specific solutions to the general problems of the appearance and the structuring of the city's overall forms go beyond their own programmatic premises and acquire an independent value within the context of the search to define the new components of the contemporary city.

Seven teams of MIT students presented their projects for the Boston Harbor to Tange. The one he deemed the closest to his own thinking on the subject is a megastructure with a triangular cross-section (figs. 100 and 101). Two orders of platforms are suspended from the A-frame: one faces the interior of the primary structure and carries circulation routes at various levels, while the other is oriented toward the exterior and contains houses and industrialized elements, again at different levels. Suspended from the main platform at the base of the A-frame are the three different systems of the transportation network—subway, highway, and elevated monorail—with ramps connecting this primary level of circulation to secondary arteries situated at various heights.

84   Quoted in *Architecture d'aujourd'hui*, no. 98 (1961): 58.

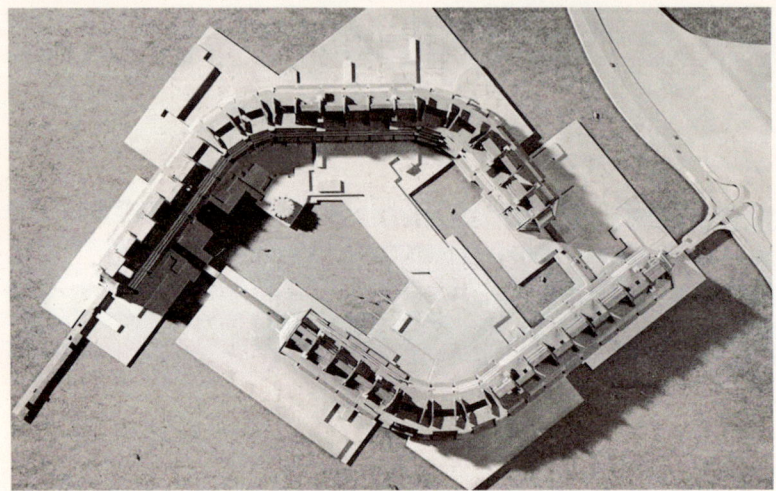

Fig. 100
Kenzō Tange
and MIT
students,
Proposal for
Boston, plan
view

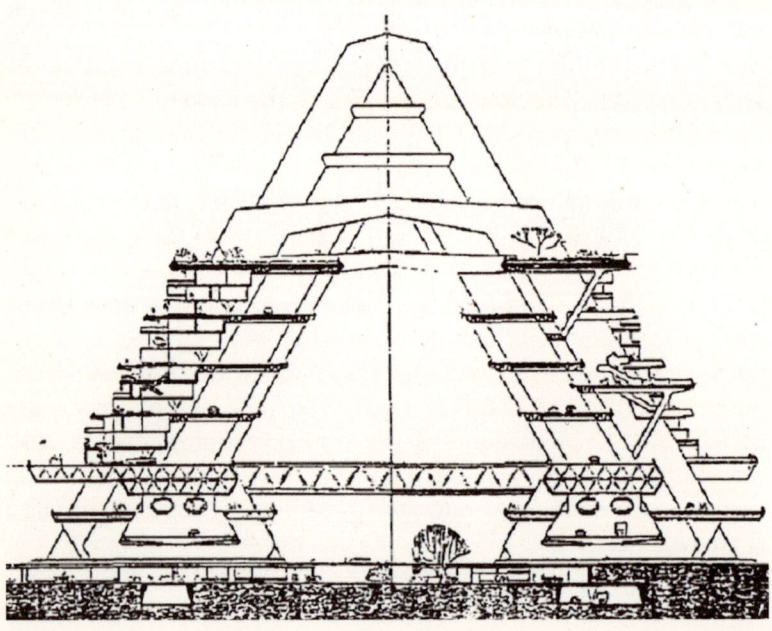

Fig. 101
Kenzō Tange,
Proposal for
Boston, section

MANFREDO TAFURI

This kind of urban organization displays a clear hierarchy of functions consistent with the theoretical premises established by Tange. The huge A-frame structure defines a new urban landscape on the scale of nature—one that orders and integrates the superhuman scale required by the new technologies, but at the same time enfolds a human scale that supports both the daily activities of the individual inhabitants and the collective life of the community as a whole.

The living units themselves are formed of an assembly of small structures that can be adapted as required. At this "microscopic" level, Tange explains, the details and the layout of the house can be reconfigured according to individual taste, allowing people to distinguish their own home within the overall "system."[85]

The system thus coordinates different scales of activity, each one with a different degree of freedom which is expressed by means of a different formal order. The scale of collective life, in the project elaborated by Tange's students, is contained in the fixed structure that specifically defines the "configuration" of the city, whereas the scale of individual human life is enabled by the organization of the housing, which allows for the greatest degree of freedom. The value of the project lies precisely in the way it integrates and coordinates these various scales of function within a single large complex. Through this, it offers a hypothesis of urban "integration" which extends to the individual level as well, with the aim of combating the sense of alienation in contemporary neo-capitalist societies.

In the light of this unabashed social utopianism, the project might appear naive, but for Tange it has an instrumental value: the importance of a study like this—which is a demonstration of an urban theory, rather than a scheme with immediate practical application—lies primarily in its instructive value for his students and for society at large. With his students, Tange erased every last trace of the traditional urban order, encouraging them to start from zero in their search for a new dimension of

---

85    See Kenzō Tange, "Architecture and Urbanism," *Japan Architect*, October 1960: 8–19.

the city able to respond to the breadth and scale of social and economic developments in our times. On the level of society, he wanted to encourage the search for a new order that might constitute an authentically *human* solution to the contradictions and alienation engendered by a misunderstood, increasingly pure technocracy.

There are many aspects of this study that can be criticized: the abstraction of the self-contained academic theme; the deliberate isolation from the existing city on the shores of the bay, and indeed from any contingency; and the lack of a relation to specific economic or legislative issues. All of these aspects can be justified, however, by the desire to create not a repeatable model—and perhaps not even an idea that might in time become reality—but rather a means of approaching the problems, a method able to inspire the pursuit of new, more advanced studies when society realizes the need for them.

b) *The Plan for Tokyo*. The Boston project, as we have already noted, was the theoretical premise for the plan that Tange and his research group proposed for the reorganization of Tokyo in 1960.[86] This is another utopian project, at least in terms of its limited practical application, but again it is an extremely stimulating one, as shown by the huge international interest and debate it has aroused.

The first step in this new conception of the contemporary city was a declaration of faith in the potential and value of the metropolis. In contrast to the whole British and American approach, from Ebenezer Howard to Lewis Mumford, Tange does not see the emergence of enormous urban agglomerations with ten million or more inhabitants as an abnormal phenomenon resulting solely from the imbalances of the "insensate industrial

---

86  Besides Tange, this group included Kōji Kamiya, Arata Isozaki, Sadao Watanabe, Kishō Kurokawa, and Heiki Koh. Tange's approach to architecture and urbanism is the most interesting aspect of his latest works. Seeing architecture as a "science" and consequently submitting it to rigorous analysis is something architects can no longer avoid, and in ths regard Tange demonstrates that a slight detachment from the contingent is at times a necessary premise for a scientific approach.

town." Rather than an evil to be cured with more or less utopian proposals that negate the very structure of the city, the metropolis is for him a remarkable qualitative leap forward that calls into question current methods of urban regulation. For Tange, the chaos and paralysis that beset Tokyo and other large cities are caused by the inability of existing means of intervention to cope with the current rate of expansion. He insists that the social and economic change resulting from the ongoing technological revolution is not to be condemned in itself, as it tends to create greater levels of freedom: the problem, rather, is how to regulate this change through a mechanism that makes the technological revolution more human and progressive.

In this regard the most pressing issue, in terms of its profound impact on the very structures of society, is to provide the *mass communication* required by the huge growth of production and distribution typical of all the new economic cycles. The segment of the population affected by these economic cycles (the "tertiary industrial population") has grown considerably in recent decades. Big cities are increasingly becoming decision-making centers that define the economic direction and organization of entire regions or, as in the case of Tokyo, an entire nation. Tange writes:

> What I speak of as an organization is not a single enterprise. It is neither fixed nor closed. It is the type of organization that results from the invisible network of communications produced by the technological revolution, an open organization in which any combination of function and function, of function and man, and of man and man is possible. By virtue of this organization, the individual functions go together to form the comprehensive function of a city of ten million inhabitants.[87]

---

[87] Kenzō Tange Team (Kenzō Tange, Arata Isozaki, Kōji Kamiya, Heiki Koh, Noriaki Kurokawa, and Sadao Watanabe), "A Plan for Tokyo," *Japan Architect*, April 1961: 10 (translated by Charles S. Terry).

The network of communications is the basic component of urban organization, with the capacity to freely integrate the social functions that the development of production tends to atomize. By reconfiguring both direct communications (roads, railways, subways, etc.) and indirect communications (telephone, telegraph, etc.), it is possible to create a higher degree of freedom in the exchanges that characterize the new dimension of the city—to make the city an open system, unified by its sophisticated, dense network of communications.[88]

And yet the physical structure of modern cities, and of Tokyo in particular, hardly has the capacity to provide for this new dimension of the city: Tange's proposal is thus a critique of the working hypotheses and models of international urbanism, making it clear that approaches such as decentralization or the creation of new towns—the very approaches that are the foundation of official planning in Tokyo—are too limited in scale to address the sweeping social and economic changes of our times.[89]

Tange points out:

> We are not trying to reject the Tokyo that exists and build an entirely new city. We wish instead to provide the city with a revised structure which will lead to its rejuvenation. We are talking not merely of 'redevelopment' but of determining a direction along which redevelopment should proceed. Redevelopment that is not orientated in a definite direction cannot solve the problems that Tokyo faces.[90]

---

[88] In the concept of the city as an open complex we also find the terms of the current debate on the "regional city," although the configuration proposed by Tange is quite specifically defined.

[89] "We do not oppose such measures as the redistribution of factories throughout the country, the construction of satellite cities, or the removal of government and educational institutions to other locations. Such measures might in some respects be advantageous. In our opinion, however, the Tokyo that remained after these measures had been taken would still writhe in urban confusion. Furthermore, the causes that led to the city's expansion would remain in operation. Tokyo will not be saved unless we keep our vision firmly fixed on Tokyo itself. Nothing is to be accomplished by escapism; there may be open spaces to which existing installations could be moved, but the problem of Tokyo's growth would continue." Tange Team, "A Plan for Tokyo," 16.

[90] Tange Team, "A Plan for Tokyo," 16.

Fig. 102
Kenzō Tange,
Plan for Tokyo

He states that the basic aims of the proposal are:

1. To shift from a radial centripetal system to a system of linear development.
2. To find a means of bringing the city structure, the transportation system, and urban architecture into an organic unity.
3. To find a new urban spatial order that would reflect the open organization and spontaneous mobility of contemporary society.

The move away from a closed centripetal structure also entails a rejection of the idea of a "civic center," even on a metropolitan scale. In its place Tange proposes a complex linear structure, which he calls the "civic axis," as the basis for the development of the city (fig. 102). The main function of the civic axis is to structure a cyclical transportation system that supports the new dimension of direct communication, the driving force in the current phase of economic and productive expansion. The axis also condenses residential and tertiary productive facilities, absorbing the flow of some five or six million people each day. The projected population is fifteen million.

The civic axis is the linear heart of the new city, the element that unites and coordinates urban and transport functions, the essential skeleton of the new structure. The circulation system has three levels of traffic, divided in accordance with the speed of the vehicles, but connected by a series of overlapping links that serve as points of interchange. As it is made up of distinct units "somewhat like the vertebrae in the spine," the cyclical system can be gradually developed over time (figs. 103 and 104). Given its function as the essential element of the restructuring of the city, and its symbolic role as the expression of an open society (as opposed to the closed city of a closed society), the civic axis starts, inevitably, from the current center of Tokyo. A mesh of the cyclical transportation system is superimposed onto the existing fabric, preserving the whole of the historic city center while also drawing it into the development process, incorporating into the new configuration. From there, the civic axis extends out over the sea to avoid the risk of real-estate speculation and to create new spatial and symbolic values.[91]

Built out over the bay, the civic axis combines mass transportation (an overhead monorail) with private means of transport, linking to the centers of business on a national and regional scale. But at this point the problem of "the organic unification of the city, the transportation system, and architecture" arises. Tange's solution is to adopt the *pilotis* used by the pioneers of modernism, which he further develops into what he calls a "core" system, where the load-bearing columns also

---

91  "Furthermore, by building on the bay, Japan would rediscover the sea, for Tokyo, which has lost most of its coastal areas to factories, would again become a seaside city. In this way, the ocean would not only become the symbol of our economic development, but a pleasant part of our daily environment." Tange Team, "A Plan for Tokyo," 19.

Fig. 103
Kenzō Tange,
Plan for Tokyo,
commercial area

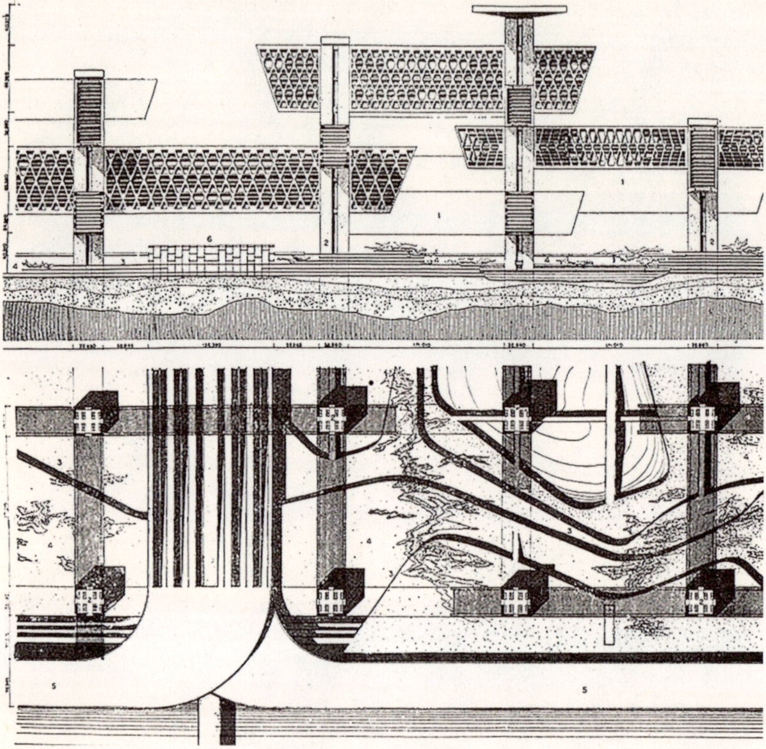

Fig. 104
Kenzō Tange,
Plan for Tokyo,
commercial area

contain the technical services (ducts, cables) and elevators. Suspended at various heights between these vertical cores are buildings with seismic walls; the walls form trusses (fig. 105). These structures intermesh closely with the overall system of circulation: their scale and their spatial arrangement are directly compatible with the complex functions of the civic axis. There is an affinity between this type of integration, achieved at various levels, and the different orders of platforms found in the MIT students' project.

In the zones reserved for residential developments, there is again a separation of the various scales of organization, differentiated according to the type of community. Tange explains the differentiation in terms of their life cycles:

There are, then, two conflicting extremes: the major structures which have long life cycles and which, while restricting individual choice, determine the system of the age, and the minor objects that we use in daily living, which have a short life cycle and which permit the expression of free individual choice. The gap between the two is gradually growing deeper.[92]

With this, the problem of reconciling planning with freedom acquires a new aspect, a new scale of values and choices. Rather than attempting to extract from the general structure of the urban organism a principle of individual freedom that can be safeguarded as the guarantor of the expanding city's *human scale*, this approach locates the exact relationship between the *human scale* and the *superhuman scale*, organically integrating individual needs into the collective dimension of the city.

The approach to the question of housing in the Tokyo plan can therefore be seen as a further elaboration of the theme of the project developed in collaboration with the MIT students the year before. Here, too, large structures with a triangular section define, through their siting and expression, the collective element of the project—a *fixed* element that does not change over time and relates, in its immutability, to the superhuman scale. But this superhuman scale enfolds, at various levels, large platforms on which individuals can construct a house according to their own taste and means (fig. 106). This ensures a maximum degree of freedom and flexibility within the large structures, which are linked into a branching system of connections between the various nodes in the city.

What aspects of Tange's project are of interest to the international debate? The Plan for Tokyo can be seen, above all, within the framework of the attempts that have been going on for some time now to define a new operative dimension in the field of urbanism. After the experiments with formulas and models that

92    Tange Team, "A Plan for Tokyo," 32.

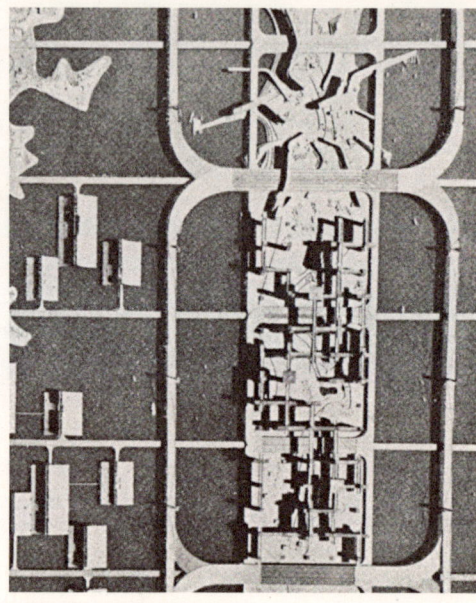

Fig. 105
Kenzō Tange,
Plan for Tokyo,
detail of the
civic axis and
residential core

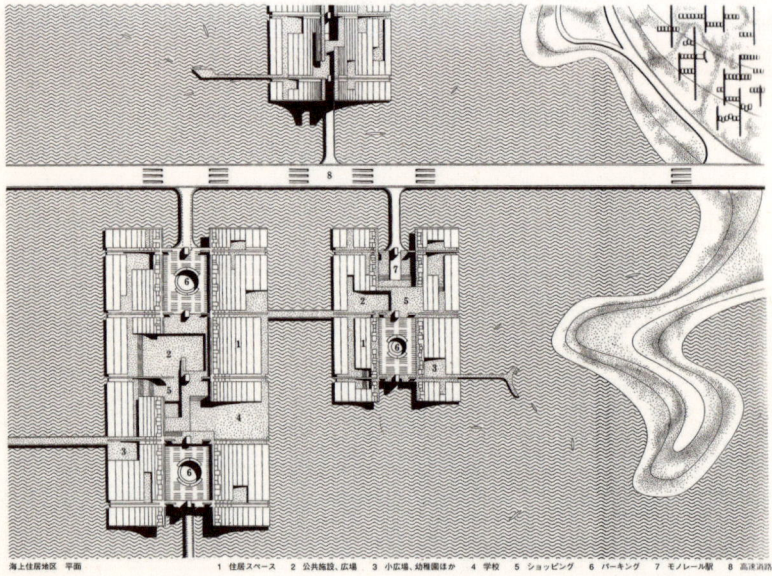

Fig. 106
Kenzō Tange,
Plan for Tokyo,
plan of a residential zone

MANFREDO TAFURI

turned out in the end to be culturally fragile or, at the very least, inadequate as working tools, we are witnessing a *redemption of utopia* on the international scene. Tange's work is one of the most vital and suggestive examples of this phenomenon.

It is significant that this redemption of utopia is particularly evident in countries dominated by mass capitalism, where the functional planning and implementation of the processes of production are creating ways of living that are far removed from the ideal or the utopian. The "form" of the city, as defined by international urban theory, has been unable to regulate the rapid growth of today's gigantic urban agglomerations; it has failed as an instrument for controlling social and political processes, as a means of interpreting or anticipating living and social structures. Besides a skepticism toward the established methods of modern city planning, this has engendered an intense search for new scales of intervention, new ways of organizing territories, new spatial dimensions, along with a new expressiveness that brings to light, magnifies, the typical features—both good and bad—of the contemporary urban condition.

The redemption of utopia is thus a redemption of expressiveness; but every utopia is also an attempt to overcome, by some contrivance, a problem that seems impossible to solve by conventional means. Tange's work is no exception in this regard. Its positive quality, its value, lies not in its possibilities for implementation, but rather in its potential to inspire new lines of thought on the ongoing cultural, political, and economic transformations.

Tange himself acknowledges as much when he warns that his proposals cannot be implemented within the framework of the current political system:

> The sectionalism that prevails in the government and in the bureaucracy prevents the birth of any comprehensive policy ... The difficulty is not merely lack of ability on the part of bureaucrats or lack of foresight on the part of politicians. Under the present illogical system, the politicians and bureaucrats could do little, and unless the system

> and organization are changed, Tokyo will not be saved. Furthermore, it is impossible to expect the force for this change to come from within the system and organization. The force must come from without and in the form of public opinion ... We believe that people of all classes and callings must grapple aggressively and constructively with the problem of recreating Tokyo. We pray that the plan we have put forward may do something to increase the interest of people at large in Tokyo's future.[93]

Contained within this rather dramatic appeal, there is a profession of hope:

> We believe that the civilization and economy of the world are about to undergo tremendous development. At the same time, we cannot help but fear that the surpluses created in this expansion will be poured into the destructive consumption known as war. The wisdom of mankind must put the expansion in production to peaceful constructive uses. Construction is the hope of twentieth-century man and at the same time his responsibility to the men of the twenty-first century. The human drive that has caused the development of Tokyo is currently working to create confusion in the city. It is precisely this drive, however, which could create a reorganized city, from which the confusion of today would be removed. We are searching, therefore, for a means to convert the energy of confusion into constructive energy.[94]

We see here how the technicians of an "organized society" are once again invoked as a force able to exploit the inconsistencies

---

93   Tange Team, "A Plan for Tokyo," 38.
94   Tange Team, "A Plan for Tokyo," 36. This question has preoccupied Tange recently and he touched on it at the World Design Conference in Tokyo in 1960, where the degree of maturity reached by the Japanese group became apparent. Tange remarked: "Reality is a movement which includes inconsistencies. To discover order within these inconsistencies and to give form to this order is our task," quoted in Boyd, *Kenzō Tange*, 18.

of that organization and validate any positive elements that might be found even in its less acceptable developments.

At this point, we can note the essential affinity between Tange's vision and that of Le Corbusier, who—in a discussion of the problems of the city at CIAM III in Brussels in 1930—promised: "Faced with the incontrovertible incontestable modern schemes, appropriate authorities will emerge. But let us repeat the chronology of events: *when the technicians formulate what they must, then the authorities will appear.*"[95] So far, the modern movement has waited in vain for these authorities.

Le Corbusier's current projects (especially the plans for Algiers and Buenos Aires) and Tange's Plan for Tokyo are consistent with this promise, in that they propose to solve a whole array of problems with a single unitary architectural intervention that is personal and peremptory—peremptory because, despite Tange's attempt to admit a degree of individual freedom, what interests them both is the absolute and didactic quality of the proposal.[96]

The validity of Tange's plan and the Japanese experiments is therefore tied to their capacity to engage directly with real-world processes and with the struggle for democratic renewal—something that architecture and urbanism can effectively contribute to, but cannot determine on their own. The risk implicit in all the young Japanese architects' urban proposals—since our remarks on Tange can easily be extended to the other groups—is in our view a risk that modern architecture and progressive culture in general should take only if they are fully aware of the consequences of their chosen course of action: in the current situation, "utopia for utopia's sake" is the most unproductive approach imaginable, but "utopia as a moral stimulus" can yield better results than "realistically" pursued operations.

---

95   Le Corbusier, "Le parcellement du sol des villes," in *Rationelle Bebauungsweisen,* ed. Victor Bourgeois (Stuttgart: Julius Hoffmann Verlag, 1931), 49, quoted in English in Benevolo, *History of Modern Architecture,* 536.

96   Many of the more interesting international studies on new urban dimensions in recent years, however, have tended to go beyond a rigid concept of time and the absolute organic unity of projects like Tange's in an attempt to revive the individuality of architectural contributions, albeit within a fixed urban fabric.

# CONCLUSION

In a memorable lecture on the major issues facing contemporary art at the present historical moment, Giulio Argan wondered if there was an authentic way to go beyond the ambiguity of an art reduced to non-signifying signs, an art that had emerged, with abstract painting, as a form of protest but also as a symptom of the failure of the whole ideological program of the modern movement, appearing as a kind of "theory of individuality as guilt."[97] He cautioned against the all too easy path of a return to reason, to the "formal rationalism of constructivism," pointing out that "such a call to order would be all the more futile as

---

[97] This and following quotes from the lecture are from Giulio Carlo Argan, "I grandi problemi dell'arte contemporanea," lecture at the Galleria nazionale d'arte moderna, Rome, December 4, 1960 (Archive source: GNAM 4-12-1960 6).

it is impossible to resuscitate the hopes that accompanied that rationalist program so many years ago, and that have been mercilessly destroyed by the events of history."

But he also noted there was another myth that had to be resisted: the myth "of spontaneity, of the revival of the organic unity of being, of a magical communion with reality, of a condition that should no longer be said to be natural—ultimately, of the possibility of intuiting the *alternative* truth of an authentic existence that lies beyond real experience, a truth that can never become experience because it is already beyond experience."

Argan went on to propose a return to the methodology of Paul Klee, who had sought to:

> uncover the incontrovertible reality of the image, something which is inherent in our existence, and affirms it against the abstraction of form… And in the image and symbol he finds an autonomous form of knowledge, one that has been used forever and is still in use today, even in our European culture, despite the prevalence of empiricism and positivism, because the form is itself, in the end, an image—the image of the European myth of reason … In making image, rather than form, the supreme value of art, Klee, like Husserl and Heidegger in philosophy, reopened a dialogue with non-European civilizations, and especially oriental culture, at a historical moment when that dialogue was seen—by all those who had eyes to see—as vital for the survival of European culture. From that moment, art no longer recognized limits or boundaries defined by nations or traditions and developed in a similar, if not identical, direction around the world.

With this we come back to the major theme that we raised in the introduction, using Sartre's words: that of the contradictory unity of culture. In the framework outlined by Argan, this unity takes on new dimensions with the developments in modern Japanese architecture and urbanism.

If it is true that the future task of international art is to search for a constructive approach that can operate without recourse to utopias or myths rooted in the Enlightenment—if it is true that the moment has finally come for the modern movement to go back to working in its own constructive dimension (just as the search for a *new constructivism* appears to be the main task of painting today)—then the first misunderstanding it needs to avoid is the illusion that such a renewal can take place without a clear ideological remit. The larger responsibilities of the arts have not been negated by the historical failure of the ideological aims of the modern movement, at least in the form they took between the two wars.

The Japanese response to all of these issues offers many lessons for European culture. In the *critical constructiveness* of Maekawa, Tange, Ōtaka, and Kikutake we see a way of bringing to the fore the idea of architectural "form" as an expression that is rich in ideological implications. This does not mean a complete correspondence between a particular form and an ideology. Rather, architecture is for them the result of a methodological process which sees the *image* as a primary tool of knowledge and communication, and this image is often symbolic, as the symbol is a means of reconnecting with an experience of the past that is replete with constructive potential for the present.

In analyzing the approach of the architecture of the Japanese new school, we have drawn attention to the aspects that are of international interest, but we have also tried to recognize the limits of their work and the less valid aspects that might suggest a regression. We might add that the redemption of the image, in all its aggressive expressiveness, might ultimately turn out to be escapist. Maekawa's and Tange's statements on this subject might reassure observers who have only a distant connection to the reality of living and working in Japan, but a look at the broader discourse suggests the need to be wary of an all too easy shift from the misconception of *revolution through technology* to the no less harmful misconception of *revolution through the image*.

We have established the limits of the Japanese experience at the level of urbanism while acknowledging both the constructive value and the inherent dangers of utopias. In a general discussion such as this, it should be added that the emergence in Japan of an *academy of utopia* speaks of a desire for escapism that is commonly found amongst those who are blocked from trying out their ideas in practice and who, as a result, construct their own artificial reality, paying little heed to the impact of their actions.

The obvious danger is that the creative drive will slacken into an *alternative urbanism* that can never become experience because it is *already beyond experience*. This is the limit that be identified in the general approach, a limit that can only be partly solved within a specifically architectural problematic.

The struggle to renew Japanese society calls for much more than a rigorous artistic strategy, and the challenge facing Japanese architects is not so very different from the one that confronts the whole of international culture. They, like us, must find a way of combining social engagement and aesthetic engagement—of exploring the links and limits of two diverse but complementary types of engagement. The Japanese new school are exploring, with resolution and clarity, a series of themes that are strongly inflected by ideology, and they are doing so with a unity of purpose and energy unmatched in modern architecture in the west. The success of their efforts will be gauged by the extent to which they are able to effectively influence—to play a non-subaltern role—in the major revision of social values that is still underway in Japan.

# SELECTED BIBLIOGRAPHY

1. For relations between eastern art and European avant-garde movements, see:

- C. L. Ragghianti. *Mondrian e l'arte del XX secolo.* Milan, 1962.
  Especially the chapter "Il contenuto storico della sintesi matura: l'architettura dell'Estremo Oriente," and various works cited in the notes.

2. For evidence of the nineteenth-century European interest in Japanese art, see:

- C. Dresser. *Japan: Its Architecture, Art and Art Manufacturers.* London, 1882.
- E. S. Morse. *Japanese Homes and Their Surroundings.* Rutland, 1886.
- J. Brinckmann. *Kunst und Handwerk in Japan.* Berlin, 1889.
  The last two are particularly interesting for their influence on art nouveau.

3. For critical studies of the history of the Japanese tradition, see the now classic works:

- T. Yoshida. *Das Japanisches Wohnhaus.* Berlin, 1935.
- B. Taut. *Nippon mit europäischen Augen gesehen.* Tokyo, 1934.
- B. Taut. *Japans Kunst.* Tokyo, 1936.
- B. Taut. *Fundamentals of Japanese Architecture.* Tokyo, 1936.
- B. Taut. *Houses and People of Japan.* Tokyo, 1937.

4. For the architecture of the Meiji period, in addition to the general works cited below, see:

- K. Abe. *Meiji Architecture, Japanese Arts and Crafts in the Meiji Era.* Edited by N. Uyenu and R. Lane. Tokyo, 1958.
- Shin' Ichi Tani. "Giapponesi scuole e tradizioni." In *Enciclopedia universale dell'arte*, vol. VI. Florence, 1960.
- E. Inagaki. "Revolt and Conformity in Architecture." In *This is Japan*, 1963; also in *Casabella continuità*, no. 273 (1963).

5. There is a lack of up-to-date histories of modern architecture in Japan. For general histories dealing with the modern movement that include Japanese architecture, see:

- L. Benevolo, *History of Modern Architecture*, vol. 2. Translated by H. J. Landry. Cambridge, MA, 1977.

More summary comments can be found in:

- H. R. Hitchcock. *Architecture: Nineteenth and Twentieth Centuries.* New York, 1958.
- M. Máté. *Geschichte der Architektur.* 3 vols. Berlin, 1960.
- B. Champigneulle and J. Ache. *L'architecture du XX$^e$ siècle.* Paris, 1962.

6. For general works on Japanese architecture with references to modern buildings, see:

- J. Harada. *The Lesson of Japanese Architecture.* London and New York, 1936.
- J. Horiguchi and Y. Kojirō. *Architectural Beauty in Japan.* Tokyo, 1955.
- A. Drexler. *The Architecture of Japan.* New York, 1955.

7. On contemporary Japanese architecture and art, see:

- S. Takiguchi. "Giappone", in *Enciclopedia universale dell'arte*, vol. VI. Florence, 1960.
- *Seven Years' Housing in Japan 1945–52.* Edited by the Ministry of Construction, Tokyo, 1952.
- S. Koike. *Contemporary Architecture in Japan,* Tokyo, 1953. Includes a summary of Japanese architecture from the Meiji period to the postwar reconstruction.

- S. Koike and R. Hamaguchi. *Japan's New Architecture.* Tokyo, 1956.
- K. Yamakosi and I. Yamawaki. *Japanese Houses Today.* Tokyo 1958. Includes an interesting chapter on industrial design.
- K. Miyauchi. *Annual of Japanese Architecture.* Tokyo, 1960.
- U. Kultermann. *Architecture nouvelle au Japon.* Paris, 1960. Well illustrated and includes biographies of the architects.

See also:
- A. Sartoris. *Gli elementi dell'architettura funzionale.* Milan, 1941. For the Rationalist-period works.
- A. Roth, *La nouvelle architecture: présentée en 20 exemples.* Zurich, 1940. For Sakakura's Pavilion at the 1937 Paris Exposition.

8. Yearbooks:

- *Contemporary Architecture of the World 1961.* Tokyo, 1961.
- *World Design Conference 1960 in Tokyo.* Tokyo, 1961.
- *Annual of Architecture in Japan, 1962.* Tokyo, 1962.

9. Special issues of periodicals entirely devoted to modern Japanese architecture:

- *Architecture d'aujourd'hui,* no. 65 (1965). Includes articles by C. Perriand, K. Ikebe, J. Belmont, Y. Murata, and H. Kano.
- *Architettura cantiere,* no. 13 (1960). Includes an article by W. Gropius, "Architettura in Giappone."
- *House Beautiful,* August 1960. Especially the article by E. Gordon, "Shibui."
- *Architectural Record,* April 1961. Includes the article by J. E. Burchard, "New Currents in Japanese Architecture."
- *Architecture d'aujourd'hui,* no. 98 (1961).
- *Architectural Review,* no. 787 (1962). Includes the article by J. M. Richards, "Japan 1962," later published in book form: *An Architectural Journey in Japan.* London, 1963.
- *Werk,* no. 10 (1962). With articles by S. Koike, A. Ayverdi, T. Masuda, and A. Hernandez.
- *Architectural Design,* no. 11 (1962). A tribute to Maekawa with comprehensive documentation of the Tokyo Metropolitan Bunka Kaikan.
- *Casabella continuità*, no. 273 (1963). Includes articles by G. P. Calchi Novati, E. Inagaki, M. Tajima, and S. Asti.

10. General articles and essays published in western periodicals:

- C. Perriand. "Crisi del gusto in Giappone." *Casabella continuità*, no. 210 (1956).
- N. Kawazoe. "Modern Japanese Architecture Confronts Functionalism: New Buildings in Japan." *Zodiac*, no. 36 (1958).
- I. Kawahara. "Tre problemi dell'architettura in Giappone." *Sele Arte*, no. 36 (1958).
- R. Bourne. "Renaissance in Japan." *Architectural Forum*, September 1959.
- B. Zevi. "Vanno in Giappone per dimenticare Le Corbusier." *L'Espresso*, no. 10 (1961).
- M. Yamasaki. "A Humanist Architecture for America and its Relation to the Traditional Architecture of Japan." *Journal of the Royal Institute of British Architects*, no. 3 (1961).
- A. & P. Smithson. "The Rebirth of Japanese Architecture." *Architectural Design*, February 1961.

11. Although numerous illustrations of specific projects and buildings have been published in western periodicals, there is almost a complete lack of monographic studies of individual Japanese architects. We can, however, cite:

- R. Boyd. *Kenzō Tange.* New York, 1962 (with a large bibliography).
- N. Kawazoe. "Masato Ōtaka." *Zodiac*, no. 3 (1958).
- N. Kawazoe. "Kiyonori Kikutake." *Zodiac*, no. 3 (1958).

- B. Zevi. "Un giapponese contro la tradizione" [Kenzō Tange]. *L'Espresso,* no. 38 (1959).
- U. Kultermann. "Kenzō Tange." *Bauen + Wohnen,* no. 1 (1960).
- U. Kultermann. "Kenzō Tange." *Das Kunstwerk,* nos. 11–12 (1960).

Tange reviewed his own work in a talk given at the CIAM conference at Otterlo in 1959. See *Dokumente der modernen Architektur.* Edited by J. Joedicke. Stuttgart, 1961. The Tokyo general zoning plan and the urbanist issues of the metropolitan region are illustrated in *Informazioni Urbanistiche,* nos. 3–4 (1961).

12. For the projects of the Metabolist group, see:

- *Metabolism, 1960.* Tokyo, 1960.
- N. Kawazoe. "The City of the Future." *Zodiac,* no. 9 (1962).
- N. Kurokawa. "Propositions d'urbanisme en Japan." *Architecture d'aujourd'hui,* no. 101 (1962).
- F. Maki. "Group Form." *Werk,* no. 7 (1963). Also published in *Casabella continuità,* no. 273 (1963).

12. Tange's MIT Plan for Boston Harbor is illustrated in:

- *Japan Architect,* October 1960.
- *Architecture d'aujourd'hui,* no. 98 (1961).
- *Casabella continuità,* no. 258 (1961).

13. Tange's Plan for Tokyo is published with illustrations in:

- *Japan Architect,* April 1961.
- *Casabella continuità,* no. 258 (1961).
- *Architecture d'aujourd'hui,* no. 98 (1961).

14. Critical articles on the Plan for Tokyo:

- G. Grassi. "La città come prestazione vitale." *Casabella continuità,* no. 258 (1961).
- M. Tafuri. "Un piano per Tokyo e le nuove problematiche dell'urbanistica contemporanea." *Argomenti di Architettura,* no. 4 (1961).
- M. Manieri-Elia. "Dal piano aperto alla città-regione." *Ingg. arch.i Ingegneri e Architetti d'Italia,* nos. 2–3 (1962).
- B. Zevi. "Costruiranno la capitale sulle palafitte." *L'Espresso,* March 4, 1962.
- P. Moroli. "Un piano per Tokyo." *Civiltà delle machine,* no. 1 (1962).

15. For Japanese architecture of the interwar period, see:

- *Gendai Kenchiku* (founded 1923) and *Shinkenchiku* (1924).

The latest projects can be found in Japanese periodicals:

- *Japan Architect,* the international edition of *Shinkenchiku* from 1956 onward
- *Japan Design*
- *Kenchiku Bunka*
- *Kokusai-Kenchiku*
- *Kindai Kenchiku*
- *Kenchiku*
- *This is Japan*
- *New Japan*

16. For building planning issues, see:

- T. Tsushima. "Giappone." *Edilizia Moderna,* no. 45 (1950).

Several articles in *Shinkenchiku*, no. 9 (1956): J. Hayashida. "Comments on the Housing Financing Corporation's Houses";
- M. Miyazaki. "Character of Housing Financing Corporation"; R. Hamaguchi. "Image of a Family as Reflected in Room Arrangement"; and F. Hayakawa. "Popular Choices in House Plans."
- "Situazione e prospettive della città di Tokyo." *Informazioni Urbanistiche*, nos. 3–4 (1961).
- *Casabella continuità*, no. 273 (1963).
- H. Kano. "Habitation et développement urbain au Japon."
- *Rapport spécial d'experts de l'habitation et du développement urbain*. New York, 1963.

17. For relations with the figurative arts, see:

- *Kindai Bijutsu Zushū* (Modern Japanese Painting and Sculpture), 6 vols. Edited by A. Imaizumi. Tokyo, 1954.
- M. Kawakita. *Modern Japanese Painting*. Tokyo, 1955.
- *Annual of Advertising Art in Japan*. Tokyo, 1957 onward.
- M. Tapié and T. Haga. *Continuité et Avant-garde au Japan*. Turin, 1961.

# LIST OF ILLUSTRATIONS

Every effort has been made to trace copyright holders and to obtain their permission for the use of copyrighted material. The publisher apologises for any errors or omissions in the list above and would be grateful if notified of any corrections that should be incorporated in future reprints or editions of this book.

Fig. 1 Kenzō Tange, Nichinan Cultural Center. Photograph: Yukio Futagawa.

Fig. 2 James McNeill Whistler, *Caprice in Purple and Gold: The Golden Screen*, 1864, 50.1 x 68.5 cm (19 3/4 x 26 15/16 in), oil on wood panel. Freer Gallery of Art, Smithsonian Institution. Gift of Charles Lang Freer. Public domain.

Fig. 3 James McNeill Whistler, *Arrangement in Grey and Black No. 1* (*Whistler's Mother*), scheme. From Manfredo Tafuri, *L'architettura moderna in Giappone* (Bologna: Cappelli, 1964).

Fig. 4 Otto Wagner, Karlsplatz Metro Station, Vienna. Photograph: Pudelek, 2016. Wikimedia Commons. Public domain.

Fig. 5 G. V. Cappelletti, Imperial General Headquarters, Tokyo. Postcard, Wikimedia Commons. Public domain.

Fig. 6 Imperial Palace, Tokyo, grand audience gallery. Photograph: Yoshio Watanabe. © Estate of Yoshio Watanabe.

Fig. 7 *Karesansui* garden in Ryōan-ji Temple, Kyoto. Photograph: Casey Yee, 2009. Wikimedia Commons. Public Domain.

Fig. 8 Main hall of the Grand Shrine of Ise. Photograph: Yoshio Wantabe. © Estate of Yoshio Watanabe.

Fig. 9 Frank Lloyd Wright, Imperial Hotel, Tokyo. Photographer unknown. © 2009 The Frank Lloyd Wright Foundation, Scottsdale, Arizona.

Fig. 10 Main hall of Jo-an Teahouse, Inuyama. Photograph: Rekishi no Tabi, 2015. Flickr.

Fig. 11 Sutemi Horiguchi, Ōshima Meteorological Station. From David B. Stewart, *The Making of a Modern Japanese Architecture* (Tokyo: Kodansha, 1987).

Fig. 12 Sutemi Horiguchi, Wakasa House, Tokyo. From *Horiguchi Sutemi no "Nihon"* ("Japan" in Horiguchi Sutemi) (Tokyo: Shokokusha, 1997).

Fig. 13 Mamoru Yamada, Teishin Hospital, Tokyo. From Tafuri, *L'architettura moderna in Giappone*.

Fig. 14 Kikuji Ishimoto, Shirokiya Department Store, Tokyo. Photographer unknown. <http://www.oldtokyo.com/>

Fig. 15 Sōusha, competition entry for the Ukranian State Theater, Kharkiv. From Tafuri, *L'architettura moderna in Giappone*.

Fig. 16 Tetsurō Yoshida, seventy variations in the composition of *tana* and *tokowaki* shelving. From Tetsurō Yoshida, *The Japanese House and Garden* (London: Architectural Press, 1955) 96–97.

Fig. 17 Tetsurō Yoshida, Osaka Post Office. © IKUO / PIXTA.

Fig. 18 Togo Murano, Sogō Department Store, Osaka. Photograph courtesy of Sogō Company History Book.

Fig. 19 Junzō Sakakura, Japanese Pavilion, 1937 Paris Exposition. From David B. Stewart, *The Making of a Modern Japanese Architecture* (Tokyo: Kodansha, 1987).

Fig. 20 Antonin Raymond, Reader's Digest Headquarters, Tokyo. Architectural Press Archive / RIBA Collections.

Fig. 21 Antonin Raymond, US Department of State Residential Apartments, Tokyo. Gerald and Rella Warner Japan Slide Collection, Special Collections and College Archives, Skillman Library, Lafayette College.

Fig. 22 Junzō Sakakura, Museum of Modern Art, Kamakura, plan. From Tafuri, *L'architettura moderna in Giappone*.

Fig. 23 Junzō Sakakura, Museum of Modern Art, Kamakura. Photograph: Museum of Modern Art, Kamakura.

Fig. 24 Kunio Maekawa, Kanagawa Prefectural Concert Hall and Library, Yokohama. Photograph: © John Barr.

Fig. 25 Kunio Maekawa, Sogō Bank, Tokyo. From Tafuri, *L'architettura moderna in Giappone*.

Fig. 26 Mamoru Yamada, Teishin Hosptial, Tokyo. Postcard, photographer unknown.

Fig. 27 Hiroshi Ōe, Hōsei University, Tokyo. Hosei University Museum. Public domain.

Fig. 28 Kenzō Tange, Hiroshima Peace Memorial Park. Photograph: Yasuhiro Ishimoto.

Fig. 29 Kenzō Tange, Hiroshima Peace Memorial Park. Photograph: Yasuhiro Ishimoto.

Fig. 30 Kenzō Tange, Hiroshima Peace Memorial Park. Photograph: Yasuhiro Ishimoto.

Fig. 31 Kunio Maekawa, International House, Tokyo. Shimzu Corporation.

Fig. 32 Hiroshi Ōe, Miki Building, Tokyo. Photograph: 2010. <http://20thkenchiku.jugem.jp/>

Fig. 33 Yoshinobu Ashihara, Chuo Koron Building. Yoshinobu Ashihara Digital Archives.

Fig. 34 Yoshinobu Ashihara, Yokohama Women's Cultural Center. From Tafuri, *L'architettura moderna in Giappone*.

Fig. 35 Junzō Sakakura, Tokyu-Kaikan Building, Department Store and Overpass (aerial photograph). Photograph: Shigeru Onoda. © Japan Society of Civil Engineers Civil Engineering Library Committee Dobo Expo Subcommittee.

Fig. 36 Kenzō Tange, Tokyo City Hall, model view. Photographer unknown. <https://twitter.com/archisound>

Fig. 37 Kenzō Tange, Tokyo City Hall. Photograph: Fumio Murasawa.

Fig. 38 Kenzō Tange, Tokyo City Hall. Photograph: Fumio Murasawa.

Fig. 39 Kenzō Tange, Tokyo City Hall, section. From Tafuri, *L'architettura moderna in Giappone*.

Fig. 40 Tōgō Murano, Sogō Department Store, Tokyo. Photograph courtesy of Sogō Company History Book.

Fig. 41 Tōgō Murano, Sogō Department Store, Tokyo, interior. From Tafuri, *L'architettura moderna in Giappone*.

Fig. 42 Kenzō Tange, Shimizu Town Hall. Photograph: Fumio Murasawa.

Fig. 43 Kenzō Tange, Tosho Printing Company Haramachi Factory. Photograph: Chuji Hirayama.

Fig. 44 Kenzō Tange, Hiroshima Children's Library. Photograph: Chuji Hirayama.

Fig. 45 Kenzō Tange, Kagawa Prefectural Government Office. Photograph: Toshio Taira.

Fig. 46 Kenzō Tange, Kagawa Prefectural Government Office. Photograph © John Barr.

Fig. 47 Kenzō Tange, Kagawa Prefectural Office. From Kenneth Frampton, *Modern Architecture* (London: Thames and Hudson, 2020), 295.

Fig. 48 Kenzō Tange, Shizuoka Convention Hall. Photograph: Fumio Murasawa.

Fig. 49 Kenzō Tange, Shizuoka Convention Hall. From Tafuri, *L'architettura moderna in Giappone*.

Fig. 50 Kenzō Tange, Ehime Convention Hall. Photographer unknown. <twitter.com/archisound>

Fig. 51 Kenzō Tange, Sōgetsu Art Center. Photograph: Fumio Murasawa.

Fig. 52 Kenzō Tange, Sumi Memorial Hall, Bisai. Photograph: Yukio Futagawa.

Fig. 53 Kenzō Tange, Dentsu Offices, Osaka. Photograph: Toshio Taira.

Fig. 54 Kenzō Tange, Kurashiki City Hall. University of Michigan Library Digital Collections. Art, Architecture and Engineering Library, Lantern Slide Collection. LS017322.

Fig. 55 Kenzō Tange, Kurashiki City Hall. Photograph: Toshio Taira.

Fig. 56 Kenzō Tange, Kurashiki City Hall, lobby. University of Michigan Library Digital Collections. Art, Architecture and Engineering Library, Lantern Slide Collection. LS017323.

Fig. 57 Kenzō Tange, Kurashiki City Hall, boardroom. From Tafuri, *L'architettura moderna in Giappone*.

Fig. 58 Kenzō Tange, World Health Organization Headquarters, Geneva, competition entry. Tange Associates.

Fig. 59 Kenzō Tange, Totsuka Country Club House. Tange Associates.

Fig. 60 Kenzō Tange, Atami Hotel, Tokyo.

Fig. 61 Kunio Maekawa, Fukushima Education Center. From Tafuri, *L'architettura moderna in Giappone*.

Fig. 62 Kunio Maekawa, Harumi Apartments, Tokyo. <https://urbipedia.org>

Fig. 63 Kunio Maekawa, Harumi Apartments, Tokyo. <https://urbipedia.org>

Fig. 64 Kunio Maekawa, Kyoto Civic Center. <https://japanpropertycentral.com>

Fig. 65 Kunio Maekawa, Kyoto Civic Center. From Kunio Maekawa and Matsukuma Hiroshi, *Kunio Mayekawa retrospective*, catalogue (Tokyo: Bijutsu Shuppansha, 2006), 148.

Fig. 66 Kunio Maekawa, Gakushuin University, Tokyo, plan. From Tafuri, *L'architettura moderna in Giappone*.

Fig. 67 Kunio Maekawa, Gakushuin University, Tokyo. From Tafuri, *L'architettura moderna in Giappone*.

Fig. 68 Kunio Maekawa, Gakushuin University, Tokyo, facade detail of the Institute of Humanities. <https://ameblo.jp/mogmog813a/>

Fig. 69 Le Corbusier, Sketch for the National Museum of Western Art, Tokyo. © Le Corbusier Foundation. © FLC/ADAGP, Paris, and DACS.

Fig. 70 Le Corbusier, National Museum of Western Art, Tokyo. From Tafuri, *L'architettura moderna in Giappone*.

Fig. 71 Le Corbusier, National Museum of Western Art, Tokyo, section. © Le Corbusier Foundation. © FLC/ADAGP, Paris, and DACS.

Fig. 72 Le Corbusier, National Museum of Western Art, Tokyo, interior. Photograph: Tokyo Photo Art.

Fig. 73 Kunio Maekawa, Tokyo Metropolitan Festival Hall, plan of auditorium level. © Maekawa Associates, Architects & Engineers.

Fig. 74 Kunio Maekawa, Tokyo Metropolitan Festival Hall. Photographer unknown. <archeyes.com>

Fig. 75 Kunio Maekawa, Tokyo Metropolitan Festival Hall. Photograph: Yoshio Watanabe.

Fig. 76 Kunio Maekawa, Tokyo Metropolitan Festival Hall, main hall. Photographer unknown. <archeyes.com>

Fig. 77 Kunio Maekawa, Tokyo Metropolitan Festival Hall, recital hall. Photographer unknown. <archeyes.com>

Fig. 78 Junzō Sakakura, Hajima Town Hall. From Tafuri, *L'architettura moderna in Giappone*.

Fig. 79 Junzō Sakakura, Silk Center, Yokohama. Photographer unknown. <hamarepo.com>

Fig. 80 Junzō Sakakura, Civic Cultural Center, Ueno. From Tafuri, *L'architettura moderna in Giappone*.

Fig. 81 Junzō Sakakura, Shionogi Research Institute, Osaka. Photograph: Docomomo. <docomomojapan.com>

Fig. 82 Kiyonori Kikutake, Apartments in Tonogaya. Photograph: Y. Ishimoto. From *Japan Architect* 1956–57: 30.

Fig. 83 Kiyonori Kikutake, Shimane Prefecture Museum. Photograph: Public Buildings Association.

Fig. 84 Kiyonori Kikutake, Shimane Prefecture Museum. From Tafuri, *L'architettura moderna in Giappone*.

Fig. 85 Fumihiko Maki, Dōjima Redevelopment Plan, Osaka. From Tafuri, *L'architettura moderna in Giappone*.

Fig. 86 Fumihiko Maki, Dōjima Redevelopment Plan, Osaka. From Tafuri, *L'architettura moderna in Giappone*.

Fig. 87 Eiji Miyagawa, Niigata Prefectural Gymnasium. Nigata City, <city.niigata.lg.jp>

Fig. 88 Eiji Miyagawa, Niigata Prefectural Gymnasium.

Fig. 89 Masachika Murata, Shopping Center, Tokyo. From Tafuri, *L'architettura moderna in Giappone*.

Fig. 90 Masachika Murata and Yoshinobu Ashihara, Olympic Facilities. From Tafuri, *L'architettura moderna in Giappone*.

Fig. 91 Hiroshi Ōe, Tōyō Eiwa Girls School. From Tafuri, *L'architettura moderna in Giappone*.

Fig. 92 Hideo Kosaka, Kyoto Post Office and Savings Bank. From Tafuri, *L'architettura moderna in Giappone*.

Fig. 93 Studio Nikken, Otsuma High School, library. From Tafuri, *L'architettura moderna in Giappone*.

Fig. 94 Studio Nikken, Office Building for Nippon Sheet Glass Co. Photograph © NSG Group 2022.

Fig. 95 Tokyo Zoning. From Tafuri, *L'architettura moderna in Giappone*.

Fig. 96 Regional scheme of the Tokyo plan. From Tafuri, *L'architettura moderna in Giappone*.

Fig. 97 Kiyonori Kikutake, Ocean City. © Centre Pompidou, RMN-Grand Palais /Dist. Photo SCALA, Florence.

Fig. 98 Kisho Kurokawa, Agricultural City. <https://archiveofaffinities.tumblr.com/>

Fig. 99 Fumihiko Maki and Masato, Osaka, Shinnjuku Subcenter. © National Archives of Modern Architecture.

Fig. 100 Kenzō Tange and MIT students, Proposal for Boston, plan view. Photograph: Akio Kawasumi, 1959.

Fig. 101 Kenzō Tange, Proposal for Boston, section. From *Japan Architect*, no. 35, October 1960.

Fig. 102 Kenzō Tange, Plan for Tokyo. Photograph: Akio Kawasumi.

Fig. 103 Kenzō Tange, Plan for Tokyo, commercial area. Photograph: Osamu Murai. © Osamu Murai.

Fig. 104 Kenzō Tange, Plan for Tokyo, commercial area. Tange Associates.

Fig. 105 Kenzō Tange, Plan for Tokyo, detail of civic axis and residential core. From Tafuri, *L'architettura moderna in Giappone*.

Fig. 106 Kenzō Tange, Plan for Tokyo, plan of a residential core. Tange Associates.

# MANFREDO TAFURI AND ARCHITECTURAL CULTURE IN ITALY

MARCO BIRAGHI

Today, he who wishes to make architecture speak is thus forced to resort to materials devoid of all meaning; he is forced to reduce to degree zero every ideology, every dream of social function, every utopian residue. In his hands, the elements of the modern architectural tradition are all at once reduced to enigmatic fragments—to mute signals of a language whose code has been lost—shoved away haphazardly in the desert of history.
—Manfredo Tafuri, "L'Architecture dans le Boudoir"[1]

1    Manfredo Tafuri, *The Sphere and the Labyrinth* (Cambridge, MA: MIT Press, 1987), 267.

For many architectural historians, especially in an international context, the figure of Manfredo Tafuri is indelibly colored by his dire predictions in "L'Architecture dans le Boudoir," first published in *Oppositions* 3 (1974), and his brilliant thoughts on "Five Architects" in *Oppositions* 5 (1975). More generally, he is associated with the intellectual milieu of the 1970s that fueled the critical debate on architecture and brought together in an ideal "circle" the Istituto Universitario di Architettura di Venezia (IUAV) and the Institute for Architecture and Urban Studies (IUAS) in New York. Aldo Rossi, Peter Eisenman, Rafael Moneo, Kenneth Frampton, Kurt W. Forster, and many others engaged in debates and exchanged views with Tafuri's work as their yardstick.

In fact, the key to understanding Tafuri's entire career is his rootedness in Italian culture—and first and foremost Roman culture. In 1960, after completing his studies in the Faculty of Architecture at the University of Rome (the city where he was born in 1935), Tafuri joined the AUA (Architetti e Urbanisti Associati) group. Along with two of his colleagues, Giorgio Piccinato and Vieri Quilici, also recent graduates from Rome, he pursued work that was focused mainly on the "city as region." This was an endeavor—shared by Carlo Aymonino—to take Italy out of a doldrums of urban planning and regulation that had left the landscape, from the maritime coasts to the urban peripheries, at the mercy of uncontrolled overdevelopment and real-estate speculation.

Within this enlarged dimension of the city, Tafuri found his first opportunities to engage in practical projects and exercise his critical skills. At the same time, he was a teaching assistant on Ludovico Quaroni's courses at the University of Rome. Quaroni, an architect of considerable importance on the Italian scene, would become the subject of Tafuri's first book, *Ludovico Quaroni e lo sviluppo dell'architettura moderna in Italia* (1964). The book marked the beginning of Tafuri's transition from architect to historian. His models during this period were Ernesto Nathan Rogers and Giulio Carlo Argan. The former was a highly regarded intellectual architect who gave Tafuri the chance to teach a course on the history of art and architecture at the Politecnico di Milano, the latter a "pure" scholar, an art historian who had also written a seminal (in Italy) book on Walter Gropius and the Bauhaus.[2]

But it was Tafuri's antagonistic relationship with Bruno Zevi that had the most decisive impact on his early intellectual development. The two first clashed in 1964 over an exhibition in Rome, *Michelangelo architetto*, curated by Zevi and Paolo Portoghesi. The young Tafuri wrote a highly critical review, mainly attacking the way the renowned historian had approached the work of the great Renaissance architect as if he were a twentieth- century contemporary. Tafuri would continue his assault on Zevi's method of "operative criticism" in *Teorie e storia dell'architettura* (1968),[3] which established him as a major architectural historian with an increasingly broad readership (notwithstanding the fact that his style is by no means straightforward, even for Italian readers).

Zevi and Tafuri would maintain their oppositional stances for the rest of their lives, just as they grew further apart from Portoghesi's position. Tafuri's major writings in the years that followed (*Progetto e utopia*, 1973; *Architettura contemporanea*, 1976; *La sfera e il labirinto*, 1980) were all characterized by a strongly ideological re-reading of developments in architecture from the eighteenth century onward.[4] In the same vein he contributed long, dense essays—a detailed "critique of ideology"—to *Contropiano*, a journal committed to interpreting the social and economic structures of Italy from a Marxist (or more precisely, workerist) viewpoint. And it was precisely on the terrain of ideology (as applied to the history of architecture) that an

2   Carlo Giulio Argan, *Walter Gropius e la Bauhaus* (Turin: Einaudi, 1951).
3   English edition: *Theories and History of Architecture*, trans. Giorgio Verrecchia (New York: Harper & Row, 1980).
4   Published in English as: *Architecture and Utopia: Design and Capitalist Development*, trans. Barbara Luigia La Penta (Cambridge, MA: MIT Press, 1976); Tafuri and Francesco Dal Co, *Modern Architecture*, trans. Robert Erich Wolf (New York: Abrams, 1979); *The Sphere and the Labyrinth*, trans. Pellegrino d'Acierno and Robert Connolly (Cambridge, MA: MIT Press, 1987).

unbridgeable gulf opened up between Tafuri and other Italian historians, among them Leonardo Benevolo. Conversely, Tafuri's appointment to the chair of the history of architecture at the IUAV in Venice—a position previously held by Zevi—allowed him to build up his own Istituto di Storia dell'Architettura (Institute of Architectural History), which would work collectively on some of the themes he had identified, producing co-authored publications on planning and architecture in the pre-war Soviet Union and the history of the American city from the Civil War to the New Deal.[5] Tafuri's Institute attracted leading scholars all attuned to his "method," among them Giorgio Ciucci, Mario Manieri Elia, and Francesco Dal Co. From Massimo Cacciari, one of the editors of *Contropiano*, who was by then teaching philosophy and aesthetics at the IUAV, Tafuri adopted the notion of the "productivity of crisis," of the "negative" as a ground for critical thinking. From the second half of the 1970s, Aldo Rossi and Vittorio Gregotti would also teach at the same university in Venice, and Tafuri maintained close relations with them, even if they did not always agree.

From the 1980s, however, we see a gradual shift in Tafuri's ideological approach to the history of architecture, influenced by social historians such as Carlo Ginzburg but also by historians of art and architecture such as André Chastel, Arnaldo Bruschi, Howard Burns, and Christoph Frommel. Tafuri would embrace a document-based history that drew on multiple sources but remained as geared as ever toward interpretation. This new phase in his scholarly career, which produced in-depth studies of some of the "giants" of the Italian Renaissance—Raphael, Francesco di Giorgio, Giulio Romano, Jacopo Sansovino, and Andrea Palladio—gave him an even more central role in the Italian architectural world, consolidating his considerable reputation among his academic colleagues and establishing

5    Alberto Asor Rosa, Francesco Dal Co, Manfredo Tafuri, *Socialismo, città, architettura. URSS 1917–1937* (Rome: Officina, 1971); Giorgio Ciucci, Francesco Dal Co, Mario Manieri Elia, and Manfredo Tafuri, *The American City: From the Civil War to the New Deal*, trans. Barbara Luigia La Penta (1973; Cambridge, MA: MIT Press, 1983).

him as an indispensable reference point for his vast following of architects, his self-avowed "adepts." (To give just one example, in 1981 the neo-avant-garde architect and designer Alessandro Mendini put an iconic portrait of Tafuri on the front cover of *Domus*, the magazine he edited.[6])

Far from confining him to an ivory tower, Tafuri's "conversion" to detailed documentary historical research gave him the means to confront a range of complex "contexts," from postwar Italian architecture to Renaissance Italy,[7] with equal acuity. In exercising his craft as a historian, Tafuri always arrived at well-defined positions, supported by his hallmark rigor and incisive arguments. That incisiveness naturally enhanced his authority and charisma as an intellectual, but it also often led to clashes with other scholars. One example that was particularly significant, even if it was deferred over time, was his "dueling" with Rudolf Wittkower's harmonic interpretations of Renaissance architecture.

While Tafuri was alive, there was a widespread recognition in Italy of his important role (amplified by the fame he had achieved in Europe, the United States, and Japan, and by the fact that many of his books had been translated into several languages). But in the years after his death in 1994 an awkward silence surrounded his work and thought—a silence broken only by a special issue of *Casabella* edited by Vittorio Gregotti.[8] This silence, observed even in the "Venice School" that Tafuri had helped to create, would persist in Italy until 2005, and the publication of my own book, *Project of Crisis,* on Tafuri's intense relationship with contemporary architecture.[9] Since then, there has been a series of studies and conferences, an "Archive and

---

6   *Domus*, no. 618 (1981).
7   Manfredo Tafuri, *History of Italian Architecture, 1944–1985*, trans. Jessica Levine (1986; Cambridge, MA: MIT Press, 1989); Manfredo Tafuri, *Venice and the Renaissance*, trans. Jessica Levine (1985; Cambridge, MA: MIT Press, 1989) and *Interpreting the Renaissance*, trans. Daniel Sherer (1992; New Haven: Yale University Press and Harvard GSD, 2006).
8   *Casabella*, no. 619–620 (1995).
9   Marco Biraghi, *Project of Crisis: Manfredo Tafuri and Contemporary Architecture*, trans. Alta Price (2005; Cambridge, MA: MIT Press, 2013).

Documentation Center" on his work has opened at IUAV, and a number of his texts have been republished (among them, most recently, a collection of his early essays from 1959 to 1964, *Dal progetto alla storia*, edited by Luka Skansi).[10]

This renewal of interest does not simply reflect a desire to give due credit to a great architectural thinker; it also emerges from a need, particularly keenly felt in Italy, to knit together the threads of a well-founded discourse that was unraveled by postmodernism. Thirty, forty years on, students and scholars may find Tafuri's writings harder to understand—they are no longer accustomed to his form of dense, penetrating prose—but his teaching and his person still exert a considerable attraction. If young students of architecture are particularly drawn by his personality, PhD students and entire generations of junior researchers are using the legacy of his teaching as their own arduous training ground by taking up his complex "method," which analyzes a historical subject in depth, seeking to uncover its breaking points and contradictions, but at the same time to encompass its overall meaning by defining how these different aspects co-exist.

How does Tafuri's youthful book on Japan fit into all of this? How was it received in Italy? We know that Tafuri himself was—in retrospect—not at all satisfied with the work, which was in marked contrast to the more attentive documentary approach of his "historical project." Generally, however, the book was positively received in Italy, as it addressed a theme that had aroused a great deal of interest, but produced relatively little in the way of substantial analysis. One belated, rather curious appreciation of the book can be found in Mendini's editorial to the 1981 special issue of *Domus* on Japan, in which he directly addresses Tafuri:

> As you are reputed today—in Japan also—to be the leading critic and historian of architectural design, and as I was anxious to introduce this intricate material in the most authoritative way ... I asked you whether you might like to

introduce this issue of *Domus* yourself. It would have been an opportunity for an important diagnosis, useful to us and them. Unfortunately, you replied that you would rather not write the introduction … You prefer to remain silent. "As far as I can gather," you write, "a subtle link with the past is what the Japanese architects of interest are seeking. But the nature of that link escapes me, which is the reason why I prefer not to speak on the subject … Is not keeping quiet, however, also a Zen practice?" Concerning your book, *Modern Architecture in Japan,* you say that it was possible to talk about Japanese architecture at that time because it was then much the same as it was over here, and it had not yet grown so mysterious as it is today … How could I have expected from your historian's lucid conscience a rapid opinion on such a remote civilization as Japan's, when your whole attitude to things actually verges on calm despair, on a suspension of judgment in face of the impossibility of surveying the situation on an infinite scale?[11]

Mendini's final remarks can be seen to foreshadow the notion of the "weak power" of analysis that Tafuri himself would propose, in *Interpreting the Renaissance*, "as one moment in a process that leaves the problems of the past living and unresolved, unsettling our present."[12] We would like history to have that same weak power of analysis to speak—in typically Tafurian fashion—to our present as well.

10  Manfredo Tafuri, *Dal progetto alla storia*, ed. Luka Skansi (Macerata: Quodlibet, 2022). Another example is the reissuing in 2007 of *Progetto e utopia*, with a new introduction by Franco Purini.
11  *Domus*, no. 618 (1981). Translation emended.
12  Tafuri, *Interpreting the Renaissance*, xxix.

# TAFURI'S JAPANESE LEGACY IN ITALY—OR ITS ABSENCE
## FEDERICO SCARONI

1. Year zero—knowledge of Japanese architecture in Italy in the early 1960s

2022. Manfredo Tafuri died almost 30 years ago and his contribution to the debate on Japanese architecture in Italy is now rarely mentioned. And yet, he was the first Italian to write a book on modern Japanese architecture.

1964. Manfredo Tafuri published *L'architettura moderna in Giappone* at a time when there were no serious publications in Italian on the history of ancient or medieval Japanese architecture.[1] Italy was one of the last countries in Europe to show any interest in this field; it had never had an intermediary between east and west—the role played by Le Corbusier for France, by Frank Lloyd Wright and Antonin Raymond for the United States, and by Bruno Taut for Germany. The few works on Japanese architecture published in Italy before the early 1960s were almost all translations of works by foreign scholars and, if the authors were Japanese, the translations were second-hand, from the English, French, or German versions.[2]

It was the huge cultural and media impact of Kenzō Tange's 1960 plan for Tokyo, first in the United States and then in Europe, that stirred Italians into looking at developments in the far east for themselves. Numerous articles and special issues of journals on contemporary Japanese architecture and urban planning were published between 1961 and 1963, many of them under the guidance of Leonardo Benevolo.[3] Manfredo Tafuri, by then an important figure within the youngest and most active group of Italian critics, was among those who wrote for Benevolo. Together with his colleagues from the Architetti e Urbanisti Associati (AUA) group,[4] Tafuri was highly critical of the Italian architectural establishment, represented by Saverio Muratori. This opposition was not only political, but took aim at the self-referential approach to architectural theory and composition, proposing instead a vision of architectural research that was more open to new points of view and different ideas

1  Among the few Italian publications that dealt with Japanese historical architecture (even if only in passing) are: *L'architettura: americana, egiziana, cinese e giapponese, assira e persiana, indiana, fenicia, druidica* (Milan: Sonzogno, 1931) and Ernesto Allegri, *Il giardino giapponese* (Florence: M. Ricci, 1943).
2  The most popular books translated into Italian included Toyo Itō, *Architettura giapponese* (Milan: Silvana editoriale d'arte, 1963) and William Alex, *L'Architettura giapponese* (Milan: Rizzoli, 1963).
3  See, for example, the chapter on Japanese architecture in Leonardo Benevolo, *Storia dell'architettura moderna* (Bari: Laterza, 1960) and articles such as Kenzō Tange et al., "Un piano per Tokyo," *Casabella-Continuità*, no. 258 (1961); Giorgio Grassi, "La città come prestazione vitale," *Casabella-Continuità*, no. 258 (1961); Kenzō Tange, "Piani di ristrutturazione di Tokio," *Informazioni Urbanistiche*, nos. 3–4 (1961); Manfredo Tafuri, "Un piano per Tokyo e le nuove problematiche dell'urbanistica contemporanea," *Argomenti di architettura*, no. 4 (1961): 70–77; Piero Moroli, "Un piano per Tokio," *Civiltà delle macchine*, no. 1 (1962); and the monographic issue of *Casabella-Continuità*, no. 273 (1963).
4  From 1959 to 1963, Tafuri was a member of the Architetti e Urbanisti Associati (AUA) group, together with L. Barbera, S. Bracco, A. Calza Bini, E. Fattinnanzi, M. La Perna, C. Maroni, G. Moneta, G. Piccinato, V. Quilici, and M. Teodori.

from around the world. Acting on this impetus, in 1964 Benevolo launched a new series of guides to international architecture under the rubric of "L'architettura contemporanea" for the publishers Cappelli.[5] The first volume was to be on modern architecture in Japan, and the chosen author was Tafuri, who had previously published articles on the subject in *Argomenti di Architettura* (no. 4, 1961) and *Casabella-Continuità* (no. 273, 1963). Drafted from the end of 1963 to mid-1964, the book was finally published in November 1964, a few months after the Tokyo Olympic Games had introduced contemporary Japanese architecture to an international audience and elevated Tange to the Olympus of the most world's influential designers, paving the way for numerous collaborations with Italian clients, notably the Bologna Trades Fair.[6]

## 2. A first small bridge from Japan to Italy, prematurely written off by its creator

For Italians, Tafuri's book was an important, perhaps fundamental, source of information about contemporary Japanese architecture, anticipating the influence that figures such as Tange and Arata Isozaki would later have on the Italian scene, and particularly on the avant-garde. But even though it had a fairly wide domestic circulation, largely prompted by curiosity about the first volume in a new series, and addressed a theme of growing interest to an Italian readership, it was not developed further or reprinted. This was rather unusual, as most of Tafuri's works went through several reprints and he liked to reprise his favorite themes and reformulate his thoughts in new or revised editions of his works. He did not, however, return to Japanese architecture, at least not in the same all-encompassing way he

---

5 Other volumes in the series focused on contemporary Scandinavian, French, Soviet, and German architecture. These were authored by Stefano Ray, Giorgio Piccinato, Vieri Quilici, and Giovanni Klaus Koenig, respectively.

6 See "Kenzō Tange per Bologna," *Parametro*, no. 1, 1970.

had done in 1964. Indeed, in a bonfire of the vanities moment some years later, he would disavow the book along with several other works.[7] By then, he had also abandoned his practice as a designer—an aspect of his formation that was undoubtedly crucial for the analysis of innovative Japanese projects that he had not been able to see in person. The macro-architectures explored by Tange and the Metabolists—similar to the projects of the English group Archigram—were clearly and favorably described in Tafuri's 1964 book. But he would later reject these projects, just as he dismissed the megastructures that emerged from the Florence-based Radical architecture movement of the late 1960s and early 1970s. The new Tafuri, historian and critic, could not brook the survival of a work so far removed from his current position.

Nonetheless, an important seed had been sown. Inspired by Tafuri's book, the Florentine architect Paolo Riani—who lived and worked in Japan from 1965 to 1971—organized photographic exhibitions to raise interest in Japanese architecture. One was hosted by the Japanese Cultural Institute in Rome in 1966; another was held at the Orsanmichele, Florence, in 1969.[8] New texts by Tange were translated into Italian, along with less up-to-date books by foreign authors, such as Walter Gropius' 1955 work on Japanese architecture.[9] Even if it rode a general wave of interest in the country following the 1964 Tokyo Olympics, Tafuri's book clearly contributed to the growing interest in the modern architecture of Japan.

---

[7] Tafuri was in the habit of removing from the IUAV library old publications that he considered superseded by his latest theoretical work. See Manuel Orazi, "La scuola di Tafuri: 'Storia e Mito' trent'anni dopo," *Ananke,* no. 80 (2017): 20–23.

[8] Istituto giapponese di cultura, *Mostra fotografica sull'architettura giapponese 1966* (Tivoli: Picchi, 1966); Consolato generale del Giappone, *Mostra fotografica sull'architettura giapponese 1966* (Legnano: Arti grafiche L. Landoni, 1966); Paolo Riani, *Architettura Giapponese Contemporanea – Contemporary Japanese Architecture* (Florence: Orsanmichele, 1969); and Paolo Riani, *Kenzō Tange* (Florence: Sedea Sansoni, 1969).

[9] Walter Gropius, *Architettura in Giappone* (Milan: Görlich, 1965); *Perspecta,* no. 3 (1955): 9–80; and Kenzō Tange, "Compiti e strutture nuove per una comunità nuova," *Chiesa e Quartiere,* no. 44 (1967).

## 3. The merits of Tafuri and his "little book"

Seen from a contemporary perspective, Tafuri's book has many shortcomings. The language is at times immature, convoluted, especially in the passages where he is attempting to describe the evolution of Japanese society and culture from the Meiji to the Showa periods and explain how this might have affected the development of architecture. Almost all the sources are foreign: *Architecture d'aujourd'hui*, *Zodiac*, *Architectural Review*, and second-hand translations of Japanese texts lifted from *Japan Architect* or *Shinkenchiku*. The lack of direct sources draws attention to the hasty drafting of the book—a haste that is also reflected in its many errors, both contextual and formal, which have been analyzed by a number of authors.[10] Nonetheless, Tafuri's work has several merits, largely deriving from the fact it was the first single-volume mass-market book in Italy to address the theme of modern Japanese architecture. In this context, and bearing in mind the absolute dearth of publications on the subject before the early 1960s, its commendable features include (but are not limited to) the following:

> ‣ For the first time, the chronological development of Japanese modernism was explained in a coherent way, allowing the architecture of the Meiji and Taisho periods in particular to be seen in a larger frame that went beyond the superficial, "poster-like" presentation of the 1963 special issue of *Casabella-Continuità*.[11] Architects such as K. Ishimoto, S. Horiguchi, and M. Takizawa, members of the Secessionist movement of the early 1920s, finally secured a place in Italian historiography, as did the journal *Gendai Kenchiku*, a bridge to subsequent developments.

10   Ken Tadashi Oshima's contribution to this volume is representative in this regard.
11   This refers to the fact that in the special 1963 issue of *Casabella-Continuità* the entire architecture of the Meiji period was reduced to a double-page collage of works with scant information on the individual architects.

- Junzo Sakakura was justifiably included in a triad of great masters, alongside Kunio Maekawa and Kenzō Tange. Togo Murano was given almost as much attention. Although these names are now taken for granted in Italian publications, they were virtually unknown in the early 1960s and would remain so for a long time to come. The authoritative *Encyclopaedia Treccani* would only get around to publishing an entry on Sakakura in 1981.

- The chronological ordering of the book was devised by Tafuri himself, and appears highly competent even by today's more exacting standards. The same cannot always be said of his critical analysis of the featured works, which is sometimes marred by his projection of an immature political vision onto the design methods of various architects, Tange and the Metabolists in particular. For all this, Tafuri's reading remains the most coherent Italian critical overview of modern Japanese architecture to this day.

- Though some have labelled Tafuri's book neo- or post-colonialist,[12] it deserves credit as the first widely circulated work in Italy (and one of the first in Europe) to ascribe to the modern architecture of a non-western country the kind of dignity that up to then had been reserved solely for western architecture.

These merits may not cancel out the shortcomings of a now dated work, but they do highlight its groundbreaking role, which regrettably has been almost forgotten in the years since.

12  Many accused Tafuri of overlooking Tange's role as a "regime designer" during the imperial period of World War II. For allegations of post-colonialism, see Esra Akcan, "Manfredo Tafuri's Theory of Architectural Avant-Garde," *Journal of Architecture* 7, no. 2 (2002): 135–70.

## 4. The lack of an heir

Interest in Japanese architecture has never waned in the decades since the publication of *L'architettura moderna in Giappone*, but to this day no author willing to follow up Tafuri's work has come forward. Even more curious is the fact that in the almost thirty years since Tafuri's death there has been no attempt to reprint the 1964 book. This is certainly understandable in other countries, in France or Japan, say, as the book's language and critical approach are now quite dated, so its importance is primarily historiographical. In Italy, however, the absence of a new edition seems more connected to the general trend to belittle Tafuri's work—a *damnatio memoriae* that began very soon after his death. Since the end of the 1990s, especially in Italy, critics have divided into two factions: an ever-dwindling number of Tafuri admirers, and a growing number of anti-Tafurians who more or less deliberately disregard his legacy. In this context, the scholarly analysis of Tafuri's work has become a niche activity for the faithful. Most of the conferences devoted to his work are held abroad,[13] while universities such as La Sapienza in Rome and, most strikingly, his own institution, the IUAV in Venice, devote little space to new research and studies on Tafuri.[14] In a cultural context of fragmentation and oblivion, it may seem normal that a book forgotten by its own author would also disappear from the public consciousness. What is much harder to understand, however, is the lack of an heir willing to take up the challenge of producing a new "Modern Architecture in Japan" —one that is updated, chronologically and critically, to respond to a country that is now totally different from the Japan that Manfredo Tafuri knew through the pages of mid-twentieth-century journals and books.

13  See, for example, the conference titled "The Critical Legacies of Manfredo Tafuri" held at Columbia University in 2006, which was followed in Italy by the online publication of a collection of short critical essays edited by Peter Lang, some of which are more intent on burying Tafuri's work than seriously exploring it: http://architettura.it/instant/20070414/index_en.htm

14  Orazi, "La scuola di Tafuri."

# THE KNIGHT'S MOVE
## CATHERINE INGRAHAM

One particular phrase from *The Sphere and the Labyrinth* (1987) stands out in my recollection of how Manfredo Tafuri's work entered the American architectural scene in the latter part of the twentieth century.

> Like the discontinuous, L-shaped move of the "knight" in chess, the semantic structure of the artistic product executes a "swerve," a sidestep, with respect to the real, thereby setting in motion a process of "estrangement" (Bertolt Brecht understood this well) and organizing itself as a perpetual "surreality."[1]

1    Manfredo Tafuri, "The Historical Project," in *The Sphere and the Labyrinth: Avant-Gardes and Architecture from Piranesi to the 1970s*, trans. Pellegrino d'Acierno and Robert Connolly (Cambridge, MA: MIT Press 1992), 16. All subsequent citations in this brief essay are taken from pages 1–17 of this edition.

Tafuri's work was already known to a number of architects and critics when he first visited the United States in the 1970s. It was in the early 1980s, however, that his work began to connect in significant ways with architectural history, theory, and practices that had emerged from structuralist and linguistic paradigm shifts and post-structural philosophy in Europe. The "knight's move" described in the above citation, which Tafuri attributed to Viktor Shklovsky's analysis of poetic language, became a central figuration in Tafuri's response to these developments.

Tafuri generally dismissed the uptake of post-structural/deconstructive theories by American architects and theorists as self-serving "language games" that, in his view, had little interest in contending with the endemic problems facing societies or redressing the subservience of architectural work to capitalist protocols. The swerve of the knight's move is, as noted, a swerve from the *real*, meaning a move away from the *works* of architecture to "what is other to it, between the object and its conditions of existence, of production, of use." Beginning in the late 1960s and continuing through the 1990s, the *real*—the works, objects, bodies, events, and scenes that we think we know when we see them or touch them or own them—was called into question by post-structural critical theory. Necessarily, philosophical contentions concerning the status of reality also raised questions about how histories of cultures were to be understood and conveyed. Along with the *real*, then, the practice of history was also called into question. For many disciplines, including architecture, these critiques of traditional methods and meanings constituted a crisis that required attention. Tafuri sought, during this period, to find non-essentialist ways of standing by the *real* and restructuring the writing of history by taking account of the evidence (brought forth by these critiques) of plurality and dissemination in multiple aspects of his subject matter—in history, language, writing, architectural production, capitalism, technology, and politics. The L-shaped figuration of the knight's move also assisted in articulating the operation of historiographic processes—histories that reflect on their own methods while arguing for a particular interpretation of the past.

Other concurrent figurations come to mind: Jacques Lacan's *gap*, for example, which refers to how we imagine ourselves as an "orthopedic whole" and yet are alienated, distanced, from the world; or Derrida's notion of the *trace* that lies inside language. However, these concepts do not anticipate the moments of "moving on" or "making compromises" that Tafuri suggests are possible after "shattering history." Neither do they result in the often-feared disintegration of our personhood or our ability to understand.

*The Sphere and the Labyrinth* proposes a "dialectic historiography" (Fredric Jameson's definition of Tafuri's method) that acknowledges the disruption of classical history and the dominance of modernism in the direction of the knight's move, which upsets the normative linearity of the game's rules but then returns to its proper place. In other words, the knight's move, a step aside that jumps over intervening pieces, immediately regains its identity and poise upon landing as a player in a complex game.

This could be described, in some sense, as Tafuri's willingness to test the temperature of the water but not to swim in it. There is, too, a certain dread apparent in his remarks about post-structural theory. One should not attempt, he warns, "to traverse endlessly 'interrupted paths,' only to stop at the edge of the enchanted forest of language." "What guarantee do I have," he asks, "that, after breaking up and dissociating stratifications that I recognize as already plural in themselves, I will not arrive at a dissemination that is an end in itself? In fact, by instituting differences and disseminations, as Derrida does, I actually run the risk of encountering the 'annihilation' predicted and feared by Nietzsche."

Nor did Ferdinand de Saussure's seminal description of language as "a system of differences without positive terms" impress Tafuri as a sufficient reason for foregrounding linguistic theory in relation to architecture. The case for this relationship lies in Derrida's focus on language as always already written and, thus, thought. Confronted with architecture, Derrida immediately proposed the need for understanding "architectural thinking." In architectural work, acts of design compose a building in advance of its construction. These are techno-intellectual acts that draw on precedents, typologies, and symbolic forms to, in effect, *think* the building and accordingly make possible its constructability. About language itself, there is much to say. The mute signaling of words that are grounded only by the sequence and context in which they are uttered or found is a remarkably stable, yet ever-changing, system. Its logic (and thus, its threat) in linguistic terms is not a destabilization of communication, but a realization that the signifier (word) and the signified (what the word names and points to) have no positive connection. *Door*, spoken or written in English, can be changed to *porte* when spoken or written in French without affecting the specific door in question in any way. The meaning of *door* lies in its relation to the diverse words/signifiers that might surround it in an utterance or written sentence. The thing itself, insofar as it engages our use and interest, is dependent on the ordering of these words. This lack of a positivist affirmation (of, in this case, a door) affects the status of the *real* in obvious ways. When we look at or make contact with an object, its reality depends on how we name, recognize, and categorize it; and our sharing of observations and perceptions about what the world is, and what things in the world are, is constantly changing.

There are, of course, numerous philosophical problems regarding the *real* and, accordingly, questions about the manner in which history can be written that directly concern Tafuri's defense of the historical project and his description of history as an act that shatters "the barriers that it itself sets up, in order to proceed and to go beyond itself." Suffice it to say here that Tafuri's adoption of the L-shaped swerve as a figuration of this process is relatively mild compared to what was being posed to architecture in the critiques taking place in the United States in the 1980s and 1990s. The "going beyond itself" of history borders on being an idealist resumption of poise that takes us back to what the swerve was meant to dislodge. As for the possibilities of "annihilation," Derrida often said that deconstruction was meant for us to see things in a different way, not to turn the page on philosophy or to destroy the world. The discipline of these inquiries lay in the questions they posed, which began to open architectural thinking to new ideas, not as a purposeful strategy to wreak havoc on the discipline, but as generative investigations. From these questions further questions arose, but not to infinity. Deadlines and limits always present themselves, but generally do not offer the opportunity of going beyond the complexity of the inquiry.

Tafuri knew about many of these dilemmas some time before post-structuralist ideas became "the thing" in American architectural circles and his choice to return to the concrete, in the midst of the dismantling of history, was essential to his significant contribution to architectural work and thinking. It must also be said, in deference to Tafuri's work during and after architecture's direct engagement with post-structural theory, that it is of the utmost importance that we sharpen our alertness to the intractable problems that face the world and the role of architecture in furthering or resolving these problems. But a further question (inevitably) arises about whether we can repair these problems, or even understand and express them, without venturing into the complex structural forces that bring them about—forces that are in some cases visible, but in most cases not.

# TAFURI AND JAPAN: PERSONAL RECOLLECTIONS OF TRAJECTORIES THAT NEVER CROSSED
HAJIME YATSUKA

1. Encounter at zero

Manfredo Tafuri visited Japan for the first (and perhaps the only) time in 1980, sixteen years after publishing *L'architettura moderna in Giappone*. He had been invited to a symposium commemorating the 400th anniversary of the death of Andrea Palladio, chaired by Seiken Fukuda, a scholar who had published an ambitious book about Palladio the year before. Also in attendance was Arata Isozaki, whose designs and writings made him the most influential architect in Japan at the time. In the 1970s, Isozaki had broken away from the influence of his former mentor Kenzō Tange and moved toward a formalism (which he called "architecture with a capital A") with an emphasis on referencing historic buildings. Exemplifying this style are the Kitakyushu Central Library and a series of buildings with vault roofs, including private houses. At the symposium, Isozaki presented a slide show of those works, for which he cited Palladio and Claude-Nicolas Ledoux as references, and Fukuda asked Tafuri for his views on this. Neither Fukuda nor Isozaki was probably aware that Tafuri had written about the Kitakyushu Library in *La sfera e il labirinto (The Sphere and the Labyrinth)*, which had been published that same year. The Italian historian's response, however, was completely dismissive: four centuries separated Palladio and Isozaki, he said, so it was meaningless to tie them together. Tafuri had cautioned against such arguments in the past, and had similarly rejected Colin Rowe's comparisons of Palladio and Le Corbusier.

I was working at Isozaki's atelier at the time, and although I was not able to attend the symposium, Isozaki asked me some days later to show Tafuri his Aoki House, one of those with a vault roof. I also accompanied Tafuri to the House in Uehara, designed by another leading architect, Kazuo Shinohara, who showed it to us along with David B. Stewart, an American historian living in Japan and the future author of *The Making of Modern Japanese Architecture* (1987). Stewart, an old acquaintance of Tafuri, introduced Shinohara as "Japan's Adolf Loos." However, Tafuri did not seem interested in this reference either. Perhaps he thought the Shinohara/Loos comparison was as meaningless as that of Isozaki/Palladio, though I personally think the comparison is valid.

## 2. Theory and practice: Italy and Japan

*L'architettura moderna in Giappone* was the first volume in the "L'architettura contemporanea" series published by Cappelli. At the time of its publication, Tafuri was part of the Architetti Urbanisti Associati (AUA) studio, which he had co-founded with Vieri Quilici, who would write *Architettura Sovietica contemporanea* (1965) for the same series, and the regional planner Giorgio Piccinato. AUA engaged in architectural and urban/regional planning that linked the morphological language of modernism with Marxist analyses of social, political, and economic indicators. The critical (i.e. leftist) assimilation of modernism through a scrutiny of historical, physical, and cultural contexts, which was fundamental to their work, shared much with thinking in Japan during the same period. In his book on Japan, Tafuri even declares that Japan had fared better than Europe in addressing its historical heritage, citing the work of Tange and the architects he referred to as the "new school." In contrast with Tafuri's later rejection of the linkage of actual works with history, as well as his lack of interest in Japan in the 1980s, one can find in this book an analysis of specific architectural works that is at once detailed, concrete, and sympathetic.

Inevitably, however, there were limits to the research that could be pursued by a young historian, still under thirty, who did not read or speak Japanese. The concept of "crisis" that became a central theme of Tafuri's later work does not figure prominently in this book, yet the same concern was on the minds of Japanese architects before World War II. Junzō Sakakura, who returned to Tokyo from Paris during the war, criticized Bauhaus modernism and averred that only Le Corbusier offered a new approach. Kenzō Tange was influenced by Sakakura during his early years, when he published his essay "Ode to Michelangelo" in *Gendai Kenchiku* (Contemporary Architecture), the journal of the Nihon Kosaku Bunka Renmei (Japanese Plastic Culture Association). Tafuri did refer to this periodical in his book, but not to the essay by Tange. This text, which is subtitled "Introduction to a Discourse on Le Corbusier" and speaks of Michelangelo's challenge to Leonardo, resonated with the rightwing romanticist notion of "overcoming modernity" prevalent in nationalistic Japanese art and culture at the time; it also influenced architects' postwar work, including their debate on tradition. This is a theme that should have aroused the interest of postwar Italian intellectuals who were compelled to confront fascism. Something else that was virtually unknown outside of Japan, but that Tafuri would surely have found intriguing, is that after the war Tange engaged in AUA-like regional planning based on quantitative economic simulations. In fact, Tange introduced and disseminated the methods of regional science that he learned about on a visit to the United States in 1959. If *L'architettura moderna in Giappone* had taken up these two subjects, it might have been an even more stimulating book.

### 3. Approaching, never crossing

After the 1973 oil shock put an end to Japan's postwar economic boom, a growing sense of crisis prompted a paradigm shift from the revised and elaborated modernism of Tange to the more individualistic poetics of Isozaki and Shinohara et al. The Metabolist critic Noboru Kawazoe, who earns frequent mention in Tafuri's book, was a theoretical cohort of Tange as well as an avowed Marxist from the 1950s on. In fact, the concept of Metabolism was derived from late-period Marx, as Kawazoe himself noted. But the ideological paradigm, too, underwent a shift in the 1970s, with the introduction of French structuralism and poststructuralism. Japan's absorption of these ideas from abroad was anything but superficial, and it was against this backdrop that Tafuri's thought was also introduced into Japan. Particularly for those on the left who balked at the consumption-oriented outlook of postmodernism, his views fell on fertile ground.

The earliest introductions to Tafuri took the form of several essays translated and published in journals. The first was "Order and Disorder," a text about Padua that appeared in the October 1976 issue of *A+U*. This included a discourse on Mario Tronti, one of the influences on Tafuri's thought; however, Padua and Tronti were unfamiliar to Japanese readers, so the article received little attention. The work that established Tafuri's reputation was "L'Architecture dans le Boudoir," which parodied the title of a book by the Marquis de Sade. It was published in English translation in the New York-based architectural journal *Oppositions* 3 (1974), then in Japanese in *Shinkenchiku* (special issue, December 1977).

I had begun writing essays and editing special issues for periodicals while enrolled as a graduate student in Tange Lab. When I read "L'Architecture dans le Boudoir" I was so impressed that I began translating and introducing other texts by Tafuri for Japanese publications like the magazine *SD*. His independent theory and historical critique were a tremendous inspiration to me. In 1981 the architect Hiromi Fujii translated *Progetto e Utopia* from the English edition, and this was followed by my translations of *Teorie e storia dell'architettura* (1985) and (as co-translator) *La sfera e il labirinto* (1992).

## 4. Shift

In 1968 Tafuri moved his base of activities from Rome to Venice, and in the course of his dealings with the journal *Contropiano* his political stance shifted in a more radical direction. His philosophical paradigm, too, shifted from early Sartre toward Foucault. At the beginning of *La sfera e il labirinto* he refers to Foucault's concept of genealogy and Derrida's deconstruction. Tafuri began to address the relationship between criticism and history, separating these from "practice" as he moved his primary battlefield from the studio to the study. His visit to Japan in 1980 came at the end of this period of transition, with *La sfera e il labirinto* being published the same year, as I noted earlier. As he approached his fiftieth year, Tafuri turned away from discourses on contemporary architecture and focused his studies almost entirely on the Italian Renaissance. Even if these subjects took the same format as two poles of his research, it is hard not to view his treatment of the first pole as a silent one.

## 5. An unfulfilled encounter

As I wrote earlier, architecture in Japan in the 1970s was marked by a changing of the guard from Tange and the Metabolists to Isozaki and Shinohara. Through his engagement with Japanese intellectual circles, Isozaki in particular swam in the new currents of thought described above, and he may well have been the first to suggest inviting Tafuri to the 1980 symposium. Indeed, the publishers of my translations of Tafuri's books were those specializing in contemporary thought, not architecture, and their readers included many in those circles. Koji Taki, a critic who at one time was a radical leftist and adopted a stance close to that of Tafuri (as well as Benjamin), was close to both Isozaki and Shinohara, and also to the aforementioned Stewart and myself. Thus, even if Tafuri viewed the likes of Isozaki and Shinohara as "individualists" at a considerable remove from the political or historical structures of Japanese society, they were in fact architects of the age of crisis. Had their unproductive 1980 encounter borne real fruit it would surely have proved significant.

After that, however, Tafuri's reception in Japan was confined to fields other than architecture. A critical practice capable of treating reality as a cultural sphere emerging from the complex call and response of society and history had not taken root in Japan's architectural academy. Moreover, practitioners of the next generation (whom I will not attempt to enumerate here) came under the sway of a regressive anti-intellectualism. This was an aspect of postmodernism in Japan, and after that unfulfilled encounter, Japan and Tafuri only grew further apart. Peter Eisenman may have argued that modernism did not take root in Japan, but a look at its political and cultural structure in the 1920s and 1930s indicates that Japan resembled Europe more closely than America did, as evinced by Sakakura's and Tange's involvement with "overcoming modernity" as mentioned above. The final chapter of *La sfera e il labirinto* was written in a somewhat journalistic style. In my view, that was because there were few if any points of agreement between Tafuri and America, at least in the postwar era. Unlike that of Japan, American intellectualism was at most a kind of dilettantism that never ventured outside the confines of the academy. Both countries were places where an outlook conducive to the *progetto* (in the European sense) at the core of Tafuri's thinking had difficulty establishing itself.

In "L'Architecture dans le Boudoir," Tafuri describes the work of Aldo Rossi as "forced continually to circumnavigate the central point from which communication springs forth, without being able to draw from that primary source," because "that 'center' has been historically destroyed." At this point Tafuri had turned his back on the contemporary and the non-European. Meanwhile, one sociologist described the situation in a postmodern Japan deprived of a grounding center as the "endless everyday." A more apt description than "postmodern" might be a non-dialectical "post-crisis" state of indifference to crisis—the most critical crisis of all. In the end, the trajectories of Tafuri and Japan nearly met, but never crossed.

## 6. European, all too European

When Tafuri visited Japan and his hosts invited him to dinner, he requested Italian cuisine instead of Japanese. Though trivial, we cannot ignore the episode for its suggestion that Tafuri may have been striking a pose of rejection of the "alien culture" of Japan.

# MANFREDO TAFURI'S PROJECT JAPAN
## KEN TADASHI OSHIMA

The project, and not only the building, is a complex tool with which one can read the layers of values deposited by society, culture, religion, beliefs and specialized knowledge; only architecture conserves these layers over time.[1]
—Carlo Olmo

"There is no criticism, only history," Manfredo Tafuri reminded us in 1986. And he elaborated, "What should interest the historian are the cycles of architectural activity and the problem of how a work of architecture fits in its own time. To do otherwise

1   Carlo Olmo, "One history, many stories," Casabella, no. 619–20 (January–February 1995): 79.

is to impose one's own way of seeing on architectural history."[2] It is important to note that this bursting of the air-tight bubble between the history of architecture and criticism—Tafuri's legacy to us—was one of the endpoints of a long ideological journey that had originated in a psychoanalytic/Marxist architectural historiography inspired by Ernesto Rogers and Massimo Cacciari in the late 1950s and early 1960s, before shifting to a structuralist and post-structuralist approach that was incarnated in some twenty books and countless articles in the 1970s.[3] By 1980, with the publication of *The Sphere and the Labyrinth*, Tafuri was presenting the work of the historian as "a work of deconstruction and reconstruction, a work which moves the connections established by Nietzsche and then re-connects them."[4] The trajectory of Tafuri's ideas was never purely linear, but rather should be formulated in the Foucauldian terms of an ideological *genealogy*. This genealogy must be deconstructed—historicized, demythified—before we can reconstruct an understanding of his impact.

Tafuri's book on modern Japanese architecture, published in the year of the 1964 Tokyo Olympics, stands out in a bibliography otherwise dominated by Italian subjects. One of the few clues to Tafuri's motivation for writing it may be found in a footnote by his Spanish contemporary, Tomás Llorens, who observed, from a distance of almost twenty years:

> Surprising as it may seem today, Tafuri had then judged that modern Japanese architecture was working along the lines of those three themes [which dominated architectural discourse in the early 1960s: the design process and its methodology; the city as the context which provides

[2] Richard Ingersoll, "There is no criticism, only history: Richard Ingersoll interviews Manfredo Tafuri," *Casabella*, no. 619–20: 97–99 [originally published in *Design Book Review*, Spring 1986].
[3] For a further account of Tafuri's intellectual formation, see Louisa Passerini "Interview with Manfredo Tafuri," *ANY*, no. 25–26: 10–69. For a selection of Tafuri's writings, see "An Initial Biography," *Casabella*, no. 619–20: 170–175.
[4] Olmo, 75.

architecture with its meaning; and architectural language as a means of symbolic communication], and that it was a positive answer to the crisis of the modern movement "because of the vigor with which it asserts its civic ideas and social contents at every level of the planning process."[5]

The crisis of the modern movement had come to a head in Italy in the late 1950s with the emergence of the "Neoliberty" group, whose eclectic and fantastical architectural forms challenged the principal tenets of the first, "heroic" period of modernism and triggered an intense debate on the dialectical relationship between history and modernity.[6] While one faction believed that the modern movement was alive and well, simply coming of age, others—led by Ludovico Quaroni in Rome and Ernesto Rogers in Milan, as editor of *Casabella*—were "engaged in a process of reassessment tainted with disbelief and heterodoxy."[7] While Tafuri was still a student, he identified with the latter faction, and particularly with Rogers' insistence that a "critical and considered review of historical tradition [is] useful for an artist who refuses to accept certain themes in a mechanical manner."[8] Also in question—and debated vociferously—was architecture's relationship with the city. Already from 1960 Aldo Rossi was lecturing on this topic and commenting on the British urban utopian movements of Archigram and Team 10 in *Casabella*. Around the same time, other intellectuals, such as Roland Barthes in France

5   Tomas Llorens, "Manfredo Tafuri: Neo-Avant-Garde and History," *Architectural Design* 51, no. 6–7 (1981): 93, note 4.
6   This heated debate was triggered by Reyner Banham's assault on the group's historicist tendencies in his article, "Neoliberty—the Italian Retreat from Modern Architecture," in *Architectural Review*, no. 747 (April 1959). Ernesto Rogers then counterattacked in the July issue of *Casabella* with "The Evolution of Architecture: Reply to the Custodian of Frigidaires," in which he affirmed Italy's commitment to modernity, but asserted that "critical and considered review of historical tradition is useful for an artist who refuses to accept certain themes in a mechanical manner." For a further description of the Neoliberty group, see Joan Ockman, ed., *Architecture Culture 1943–1968* (New York: Rizzoli, 1993), 300–07.
7   Llorens, 85. Particularly notable is the special edition of *Casabella* (no. 251, 1961) that offered a reevaluation of the past fifteen years of Italian architecture, with contributions from Rossi, Quaroni, Giuseppe Samonà, Vittorio Gregotti, and Giancarlo Da Carlo, among others.
8   Ockman, 303.

and Umberto Eco in Italy, began to shape a discourse on architectural language as a symbolic communication.

Tafuri would enter the fray in April 1961, with an article in *Ardometi de Architettura* that responded to the publication, in the American journal *Architectural Forum* two months earlier, of Kenzō Tange's dramatic plan for the urban reorganization of Tokyo.[9] For Tafuri, Tange's work displayed a "dynamism" of "incontrovertible international influence."[10] The Plan for Tokyo, as he would later note, was "a polemic against the two-dimensional tradition of planning, with its theories of territorial equilibrium based on decentralization by means of satellite towns. With Tange the exaltation of the tertiary city and the mobility of the urban structure are explicit. His megastructure summons up an entirely uncommon scale of design." What made the work particularly powerful for Tafuri was the fact that, in contrast to the utopian megastructures proposed by other groups, notably Archigram in England, Tange's plans were actually being realized. Tange had already built the Hiroshima Peace Memorial and Plaza (1952) and the Tokyo City Hall (1952–57) and was then in the process of completing the megastructure of the Yamanashi Communication Center along with other civic buildings all around Japan. For Tafuri, Tange's architecture was not only built on an urban scale, but inflected with a "mannerist quality" that addressed past architecture. It not only offered concrete solutions to many of the same architectural concerns that Italy had to confront in the 1960s, but was a positive force for social change. Tange would subsequently become one of the main protagonists in Tafuri's commercially produced guide to modern Japanese architecture. Of the book's ninety-six illustrations, which span from the sixteenth-century Zen garden, Ryōanji, to Tange's plan for the reconstruction of Tokyo, nearly half show the work of Tange or his mentor Kunio Maekawa.

9    Manfredo Tafuri, "Un piano per Tokio e le nuove problematiche dell'urbanistica contemporanea," *Ardometi de Architettura*, no. 4 (1961). Tange's plan would be published in the December 1961 issue of *Casabella*.

10   Manfredo Tafuri and Francesco Dal Co, *Modern Architecture*, trans. Robert Wolf (New York: Harry Abrams, 1979), 385.

However, Tafuri's construction of a history of modern Japanese architecture was severely limited by his reliance on translated secondary sources. Unable to read or speak Japanese, he had no means of identifying either the hierarchical underpinning of the language or the subtly shaded meaning in architectural texts. More precisely, he had no means of bringing "class criticism into architecture," as he would later do. Unaware of the dramatic transformation of the written language after World War II, when it was streamlined to make it more accessible, he also failed to note how this had helped to create a social foundation for a modern architecture.

Many Japanese terms are dutifully transliterated, but nonetheless the text is strewn with errors: the *Bunriha* (Secessionist group) becomes "Bunchika", for example, and *Nihon* (Japan) "Nihou." More than just an editorial slip, the lack of attention to *Bunriha* is an indication that Tafuri did not fully understand the role this avant-garde movement had played in the formation of modern architecture in Japan. *Bunriha* (1920–28) was not simply a sub-branch of the Viennese Secessionist group that had been founded some twenty years earlier, but was a hybrid variation, stylistically closer to the current of European expressionism. However, *Bunriha's* iconoclastic activities broke with both historical European styles, laying the foundations of the utopian avant-garde in Japan. In overlooking Bunriha, Tafuri missed the opportunity to link Tange's utopian plan and the Metabolist work of the 1960s to much earlier precedents.

Unable to interpret his objects of study through the written word, Tafuri was forced to rely heavily on images. But architectural photographs can also project a myth or be simply a canvas for preconceived notions. Tafuri himself would later warn of the dangers of "critical photography," which "risks being caught by the very devil that it is trying to exorcise: it often ends by becoming an end in itself, an autonomous image only very slightly related to the linguistic structures that it is trying to explore."[11] And the

---

11  Manfredo Tafuri, *Theories and History of Architecture*, trans. Giorgio Verrecchia (New York: Harper & Row, 1979), 157.

problem of the autonomous image would again plague him in *Theories and History of Architecture*, in which he mistakenly located Tange's Yamanashi Building in Tokyo.¹²

Tafuri's linguistic limitations also prevented him from debunking Tange's own narrative, which officially begins after the war, with the building of his Hiroshima Peace Memorial—a phoenix rising from the ashes. What is missing from this story is Tange's reactionary phase during the interwar years, when he supported the militarist regime and submitted a scheme for a memorial hall in the form of a Japanese shrine-like complex, with Mount Fuji rising in the background.¹³ Tafuri presented Maekawa and Tange as "rigorous mannerists" who were continuing themes of Le Corbusier, unaware that Tange had initially taken a historicist stance, as a foe rather than an advocate of purist modernism.

Careful to avoid orientalizing Japanese architecture, Tafuri unwittingly dehistoricized traditional architecture by lumping together four illustrations of pre-modern architecture spanning one thousand and two hundred years.¹⁴ Scanning secondary sources, he was unaware these works were part of a Japanese canon that had been constructed in the 1930s in reaction to the importation of western modernism.¹⁵ Tafuri's cursory knowledge of Japanese history was also problematic in his analysis of Tange's 1960 Plan for Tokyo. Seduced by Tange's images of a megastructure linear city, he failed to note that this form

---

12  The Yamanashi Building, a megastructure civic complex, is more than a two-hour ride by express train from Tokyo.
13  Terunobu Fujimori, *Nihon no Kendai Kenchiku: Taishō-Showa* (Modern Japanese architecture: Taishō-Showa period) (Tokyo: Iwanami Shinchō, 1993), 238–39. Tange's interwar activities—a highly sensitive issue that he himself has refused to address—are presently coming to light through the historical evaluation of his work by Fujimori and the journal *Shinkenchiku*.
14  Specifically, he starts with the Jo-an Teahouse (Momoyama period, 1568–1614), then jumps to the *Shinden*-style Imperial Palace (Heian period 782–1184), the Zen Buddhist garden Ryōanji (Muromachi period (1333–1567), and the late-seventh-century Shinto shrine of Ise (which Tafuri dates back to the fifth century).
15  Sutemi Horiguchi led this movement through a historical study of Momoyama period tea houses that aimed to identify and construct an indigenous Japanese architecture. See Fujioka Toyoasu, ed., *Horiguchi Sutemi no Nihon* (Sutemi Horiguchi's Japan) (Tokyo: Kenchiku Bunka, 1996).

was in direct opposition to the spiral-shaped, castle-town plan of Edo/Tokyo.[16] Nor did he contextualize the critical moment—the significant revision of the US–Japan Security Treaty and the double-digit economic growth—that had created a situation conducive to the plan. One could interpret Tafuri's subsequent silence about this book as a sign that he was fully aware of these failings. In *Theories and History of Architecture*, published four years later, he would emphasize "the need for deep analyses to bring out the hidden mechanisms of the use and formation of (architectural) language."[17] In that book, too, he distilled a valid and provocative conclusion on Tange, underscoring inherent parallels between the Japanese new school and "some Italian experiences, from Aldo Rossi to the neo-constructivism of Samonà,"[18] noting that what "Tange seemed to say" was: "The availability of the town allows ... some contradictions, allows the realization of utopias, allows criticism from within... ."[19]

Both Tafuri and Tange lived in countries that had seen the rise and fall of nationalist militarism during World War II, and were relatively recent constructions of a modern nation state. In the immediate aftermath of the war, historians in both Italy and Japan had to tackle the problematic legacy of ultra-nationalism. And both Tafuri and Tange had to deal with a similar architectural crisis in the 1960s. Seen from a broader perspective, both their countries were grappling with the same fundamental problems of modernity, which touched all aspects of society, of government, and of the economy. In this context, Marxist-based historiography provided a powerful instrument of analysis not only for Tafuri and Benevolo in Italy, but also for Walter Benjamin, Jürgen Habermas, and others of the Frankfurt School in Germany, as well as the modernist historian Maruyama Masao in Japan. For these historians, liberation and equality—the goals they shared with the modern movement in architecture

16   Edo was officially renamed Tokyo in 1868 with the fall of Tokugawa feudal rule and the restoration of the Meiji emperor.
17   Tafuri, *Theories and History*, 176.
18   Tafuri, *Theories and History*, 92.
19   Tafuri, *Theories and History*, 96.

—could only be achieved through class struggle. As Walter Benjamin observed:

> The class struggle, which is always present to a historian influenced by Marx, is a fight for the crude and material things without which no refined and spiritual things could exist.... A historical materialist must be aware of this most inconspicuous of all transformations.[20]

Despite the vast geographical distances between these countries, it was believed that any differences between them were not structural, but merely a matter of different stages of development. All nations, then, could ultimately be linked by the universal ideology of Marxism, which would penetrate every aspect of culture. Maruyama explained:

> Marxist philosophy and interpretation of history held not only that ... economy, law, and politics were ineluctably linked, but that even the fields of literature and art had to be seen not in isolation but as linked mutually with them. By pointing out the common foundation from which the various aspects of the "superstructure" arise, Marxism may fairly be deemed the first *Weltanschauung* in modern Japan which compelled one intellectually to explicate the transformation of social systems in a total and coherent fashion.[21]

In these terms, Maruyama, Tafuri, and other historians from a Marxist lineage were fundamentally committed to the ideology of modernity: to the creation of a true democracy—an authentic, genuinely free society.

Tafuri's and Maruyama's historiographical paradigms would subsequently shift. While Tafuri's *Architecture and Utopia* (1973)

---

20  Walter Benjamin, "Theses on the Philosophy of History," in *Illuminations*, trans. Harry Zohn (New York: Schocken Books, 1969), 254–55.
21  Andrew Barshay, "Imagining Democracy in Postwar Japan: Reflections on Maruyama Masao and Modernism," *Journal of Japanese Studies* 18, no. 2 (Summer 1992): 370.

is still inflected by a neo-Marxian perspective, *The Sphere and the Labyrinth* (1980) reflects his embrace of post-structuralism and the growing influence of Michel Foucault. Diagnosing the dilemmas of modernity and of late capitalism, Tafuri no longer discerned a "linear causality" of historical development but, in its place, a "genealogy" made up of "not-obvious truths."[22] Maruyama, too, was impelled to respond in the 1980s to the fact that modern society was not developing in accordance with the Marxist model. Despite the seemingly complete transformation of the polity with the collapse of Tokugawa feudal rule in 1868, he saw a continuity of political and intellectual thought in Japan—a *basso ostinato*, an unchanging repetitive base line, as the motif in history that does not go away.[23] Tafuri echoed these sentiments through his assertion that "architecture shows continually that the very basis of its existence is in the unstable balance between a nucleus of permanent values and meanings, and their metamorphoses in historical time."[24] Maruyama's questioning of Marxist structures would thus roughly coincide with the translation of Tafuri's polemical works into Japanese during the mid-1980s and the rise of the late capitalist "bubble period."

22  Specifically, Tafuri writes: "In effect, to link the problem of history with the rediscovery of mythical 'origins' presupposes an outcome totally rooted in nineteenth-century positivism. In posing the problem of an 'origin,' we presuppose the discovery of a *final* point of arrival: a destination point that *explains* everything, that causes a given 'truth,' a primary value, to burst forth from the encounter with its original ancestor. Against such an infantile desire to 'find the murderer,' Michel Foucault has already counterposed a history that can be formulated as *genealogy:* 'Genealogy does not oppose itself to history as the lofty and profound gaze of the philosopher might compare to the mole-like perspective of the scholar; on the contrary, it rejects the metahistorical deployment of ideal significance and indefinite teleologies. It opposes itself to the search for 'origins.'" Not by chance does Foucault base on Nietzsche his 'archeology of knowledge,' which, like Nietzsche's genealogy, is 'made up of little, not obvious truths, arrived at by a rigorous method...' To avoid the chimera of origin, the genealogist must avoid all notions of linear causality. He thus exposes himself to a risk, provoked by the shocks and accidents, by the weak points or points of resistance that history itself presents. There is no constancy in such a genealogy, but above all no 'rediscovery' and no 'rediscovery of ourselves.' For 'knowledge is not made for understanding; it is made for cutting.'" Manfredo Tafuri, *The Sphere and the Labyrinth*, trans. Pellegrino d'Acierno and Robert Connolly (Cambridge, MA: MIT Press, 1990), 4–5.

23  Masao Maruyama, "The Structure of *Matsurigoto*: The *basso ostinato* of Japanese Political Life," in Henny and Lehmann, eds., *Themes and Theories in Modern Japanese History* (London: Athlone, 1988), 27–43.

Tafuri brought to his analysis a distinctive focus on the multiple social, political, and economic values that contribute to the shaping of architecture. In *Theories and History*, he would build on Walter Benjamin's assertion that a specific quality of architecture is the way it is "appropriated in a twofold manner: by use and perception" by highlighting the complex relations of architecture to society.[25] The "intentional insertion of the artistic product into the cycle of daily life," he wrote, opened up architecture to "transformation, interpretation, and even misunderstanding on the part of the observer."[26] Architecture could be perceived either as a pure form or in its contextual totality as a "Total Theater."[27] In the latter case, understanding the totality required "deep analysis to bring out the hidden mechanisms of the use and formation of language." Although Tafuri made almost no reference to Japanese architecture after the 1960s, the central themes of *Theories and History* are in fact already present in this formative work on Japan. "In the last fifteen years," he wrote—that is, in the span between *L'architettura moderna in Giappone* and *Theories and History*—these themes had "become problems whose solution can no longer be deferred."[28]

24    This statement was written before Tafuri's paradigmatic intellectual shift, but it foreshadows his change in thinking. While there is a single reference to Foucault in *Theories and History of Architecture* (on p. 178), there are twenty in *The Sphere and the Labyrinth*.
25    Walter Benjamin, "The Work of Art in the Age of Mechanical Reproduction," in *Illuminations*, trans. Harry Zohn (New York: Schocken Books, 1969), 240.
26    Tafuri, *Theories and History*, 89.
27    Tafuri, *Theories and History*, 91.
28    Tafuri, *Theories and History*, 176.

An earlier version of this text was published under the title "Manfredo Tafuri and Japan: An Incomplete Project," in *Architectural Theory Review* 8, no. 1 (2003): 16–29.

# CONTRIBUTORS

Marco Biraghi is full Professor at the Politecnico di Milano, where he teaches history of contemporary architecture. His books include *Storia dell'architettura contemporanea 1750–2008* (Einaudi, 2008), *Project of Crisis: Manfredo Tafuri and Contemporary Architecture* (MIT Press, 2013), *Storia dell'architettura italiana 1985–2015* (with S. Micheli, Einaudi, 2013), *L'architetto come intellettuale* (Einaudi, 2019), *Questa è architettura: Il progetto come filosofia della prassi* (Einaudi, 2021), *Post Western Histories of Architecture* (with P.M. Guerrieri, Routledge, 2022). He also edited the Italian edition of *Delirious New York* by Rem Koolhaas (Electa, 2001).

Catherine Ingraham is a tenured Professor in the graduate program of architecture at Pratt Institute. She received her doctoral degree from Johns Hopkins University and has been a visiting faculty member at Harvard GSD and Columbia GSAPP. Her publications include *Architecture's Theory* (MIT Press, 2023), *Architecture, Animal, Human* (Routledge, 2006), *Architecture and the Burdens of Linearity* (Yale University Press, 1998), as well as many articles and invited essays. She was an editor, with K. Michael Hays and Alicia Kennedy, of the critical journal *Assemblage* for eight years.

Mohsen Mostafavi, architect and educator, is the Alexander and Victoria Wiley Professor of Design and Harvard University Distinguished Service Professor, and served as Dean of the GSD from 2008 to 2019. His work focuses on modes and processes of urbanization and on the interface between technology and aesthetics. Recent publications include *Ethics of the Urban: The City and the Spaces of the Political* (Lars Müller, 2017); *Portman's America and Other Speculations* (Lars Müller, 2017); and *Sharing Tokyo: Artifice and the Social World* (Actar, 2022) He is currently engaged in a multi-year research project on the future of urbanization in Japan.

Ken Tadashi Oshima is Professor at the University of Washington, Seattle, where he teaches transnational architectural history, theory, and design. He has been a visiting faculty member at Harvard GSD and UCLA. He is a Fellow of the Society of Architectural Historians (SAH) and served as President of the SAH from 2016 to 2018. Dr. Oshima's publications include *International Architecture in Interwar Japan: Constructing Kokusai Kenchiku* (University of Washington Press, 2009), *Arata Isozaki* (Phaidon, 2009), *Global Ends: Towards the Beginning* (Toto, 2012), and *Kiyonori Kikutake: Between Land and Sea* (Harvard GSD/Lars Müller, 2016).

Federico Scaroni studied architecture at Sapienza, University of Rome, where he later obtained a PhD in Design Theory. His interests are divided between research and practice. After winning a MEXT scholarship he moved to Japan in 2009 and was a visiting researcher and JSPS Fellow at the University of Tokyo until 2016. His publications include *Along the Water: Urban Crises between Italy and Japan* (Sayusha, 2017) and *Invisible Architecture: Italian and Japanese Architectural Movements in the 1960s and 1970s and the Contemporary Debate* (with R.E. Adamo and C. Lippa, Silvana, 2017). He currently combines practice in his own firm, FSADesign, with teaching at New York University of Tirana.

Hajime Yatsuka is an architect and Professor Emeritus at Shibaura Institute of Technology, Tokyo. His work as a historian and critic focuses on contemporary architecture and urbanism. He is the author of books on the Russian avant-garde, Le Corbusier, Mies van der Rohe, and Metabolism, among other subjects, and also the translator of Manfredo Tafuri's *Teorie e storia dell'architettura* (1985) and *La sfera e il labirinto* (co-translator, 1992). Translations of his texts have been published in many journals in the US and Europe. He is currently working on Soviet constructivism, as found in politics, economy, art, and urbanism.

Many thanks to all the contributors to this project: Ken Tadashi Oshima for his guidance and friendship, Kayoko Ota for her collaboration, Miguel Lopez Melendez and Qin Ye Chen for their image research, Mr. Toichi Takenaka and the Takenaka Corporation for their support of the Japan Research Initiative at the Harvard University Graduate School of Design, and finally to all at MACK for their exceptional commitment to this project.
—Mohsen Mostafavi

*Modern Architecture in Japan*
Manfredo Tafuri

First published as *L'architettura moderna in Giappone*
by Cappelli Editore 1964
This edition first published by MACK 2022

Editor: Mohsen Mostafavi
Text editor: Pamela Johnston
Translator: David Kerr
Image researchers: Miguel Lopez Melendez, Qin Ye Chen
Project editor: Louis Rogers
Designer: Morgan Crowcroft-Brown

© 2022 MACK for this edition
© 2022 Quodlibet srl for Manfredo Tafuri's text
© 2022 David Kerr for his translation
© 2022 Marco Biraghi, Catherine Ingraham, Mohsen Mostafavi, Ken Tadashi Oshima, Federico Scaroni, and Hajime Yatsuka for their texts

Printed and bound in Germany

ISBN 978-1-913620-83-7
mackbooks.co.uk